Reinventing America

Michael Foudy

☆ ☆ ☆ ☆ ☆ ☆ ☆ ☆ ☆ ☆ ☆ ☆ ☆

REINVENTING AMERICA

☆ ☆ ☆ ☆ ☆ ☆ ☆ ☆ ☆ ☆ ☆ ☆ ☆

The Institute For American Democracy Press
Scottsdale, Arizona

An Institute For American Democracy Press Book
Published by The Institute For American Democracy Press

Copyright © 1992, The Institute For American Democracy Press
All rights reserved under International and Pan-American Copyright Conventions.
Published in the United States by The Institute For American Democracy Press,
Scottsdale, Arizona.

Laser Typography by Michael Mele, Brooklyn, New York.

Library of Congress Cataloguing-in-Publication Data

Foudy, Michael
Re-inventing America

92-8633
CIP

ISBN 0-9632571-0-2

Dedication

To my daugher Erin and her generation
in hopes that they will learn from the mistakes
of those of us who have gone before, and live their lives
in accordance with/in the spirit of . . .

Wiconi gluonihan pi na wolakota.

ACKNOWLEDGMENTS

When I started this book in August of 1990, I expected to finish in a matter of weeks. Now, more than 16 months later, I have forced myself to stop writing, I hope you will find it entertaining, educational, thought-provoking, and a stimulus for action.

Needless to say, I could not have done this alone. First, I wish to acknowledge the patience and perseverance of my wife, Dorothy Simmons, who has lived through the process, provided moral support, offered important insights, and put up with the hassles inherent in any creative process.

Second, there would be no book but for the hard work, talent, and intelligence of my editor, Melody Sears. She has saved me from myself more often than I care to admit, while making sense out of this manuscript.

Third I wish to acknowledge the forbearance of all the people engaged in the production of this book. They include Ruthann Powell, Will Guilliams, Michael Mele, Greg Albright, George Lizama, Gary Tenen, Bill Sims, Birgil Kills Strait, and Marilyn Pourier.

Fourth, I thank all of those friends and associates upon whom I imposed, who graciously read what I had written and offered commentary which inevitably improved this work. They include (in reverse alphabetical order, Peter) Peter Zimmerman, Charles Pine, Brad Niemcek, Jerry Naylor, Nona B. Mott, Jack Moulton, Ann Medigovich, Jim Ludke, David Horowitz, Bill Holmberg, Jim Gjurgevich, John P. Frank, Bob Edwards, Michael Deaver, Mary Frances Clinton, Dr. Thomas Boyd, John Baines, and Polly Agee.

Fifth, thanks to those people who helped me to understand the way the world works without whom this effort would never have been undertaken, including Jim McNulty, Charles Perry, Jake Lathan, Bill Meek, Frank Callahan, and Charles Walters.

Finally, without the encouragement and support of Steve Hutchison and my parents, Michael and Olga Foudy, this book would not have been completed.

Contents

Forward

Let Us Now Try Liberty! God has given to men all that is necessary for them to accomplish their destinies. He has provided a social form as well as a human form. And these social organs of persons are so constituted that they will develop themselves harmoniously in the clean air of liberty. Away, then, with quacks and organizers! Away with their rings, chains, hooks, and pincers! Away with their artificial systems! Away with their whims of governmental administrators, their socialized projects, their centralization, their tariffs, their governmental schools, their state religions, their free credit, their bank monopolies, their regulations, their restrictions, their equalization by taxation, and their pious moralizations!

And now that the legislators and do-gooders have so futilely inflicted so many systems upon society, may they finally end where they should have begun: May they reject all systems, and try LIBERTY; for liberty is an acknowledgment of faith in God and His works.

Frederic Bastiat
"The Law"
June, 1850

Frederic Bastiat, a French anti-socialist, economist, statesman, and author, wrote of the fallacies of socialism and communism during the French Revolution of 1848. His warnings fell on deaf ears. The same socialist-communist ideals and plans denounced by Bastiat but adopted in

France are now threatening America.

I dedicate this statement by Bastiat to my friend, Michael L. "Mike" Foudy, who more than one hundred years later brings us to the realization that we have only one choice of survival as the Superpower Nation in this rapidly changing world. That choice is to "Reinvent America" and indeed "Try Liberty" again!

How did Mike Foudy and Jerry Naylor progress from our seemingly endless conversations of Rock and Roll to Bastiat, Locke, Von Mises, and the Holistic, Political, Common-Sense Domestic Agenda for America? Traveling from Rock and Roll to politics has not been an uncommon venture for Mike and myself since we first met in 1987. Back then we tried to find a common political ground upon which to establish our friendship—Mike from the Left (or so he first stated) and I from the Right (as exemplified by my avidly Conservative Reagan spoutings)—and we successfully bridged the gap, learning much in the process.

To understand Mike Foudy is to know him. To know him is to sit for hours and travel the trails of political campaigns he has tramped; the fields of farm issues he's championed; the wasteland of environmental propositions he's conquered.

Reinventing America is the direct result of releasing much pent-up frustration from my friend. Frustration which you and I, along with millions of other Americans, are currently feeling. "I'm mad as hell and I'm not going to take it any more," has become a popular rallying cry of late. Well, Mike's not going to take it any more...and neither should we.

In this book, Mike Foudy has stripped down to the basics and shared his innermost thoughts, frustrations, ideals, and dreams. He has given us the opportunity to stop and think about what we must do to get our country back on its foundation—beginning with each of us as individuals putting our own personal house in order! The text of this book is not a panacea for all of our problems. Rather, it is a stimulus designed to arouse conversation, positive exchange of ideas and, most important, ACTION! This grass-roots, common-sense approach to the problems which we are facing every day can and will make things better. It will change the way we live and it will put America back together again.

Through Mike's writings we can analyze the problems that exist in America today and fix them. We can take charge of our own destiny and that of our nation. Each of us CAN make a difference. Each of us MUST make a difference. This is Mike's challenge, and we as responsible human beings must accept this challenge. Please read *Reinventing America* and see if you don't agree.

When my Texas friend, John Howell, first introduced me to the writings of Adam Smith, Henry Grady Weaver, Albert Jay Nock, Ludwig Von Mises, Frederic Bastiat, and others, little did I think I would in turn share them with Mike, who would in his turn reawaken Americans to the basic truths espoused by our predecessors. Through this reawakening, and the personal action we must take, the process of "Reinventing America" will make the United States a stronger and more economically sound nation again. God Bless America . . . and thank you Mike!

Jerry Naylor
December 1991

Introduction

BEFORE YOU BEGIN TO READ THIS BOOK, it is appropriate to share with you both what it is and what it is not. *Reinventing America* is NOT a political manifesto, a platform for a political party, or a program for government.

Reinventing America is a personal call to action. I want you to stop allowing yourself to be the victim of forces which appear to be beyond your control. I want you to stand with me and be counted as American citizens willing to defend our way of life and fight for our children's future. I want you to make the American dream a reality for yourself, your family, your community, your country, and the world.

It is NOT going to be easy. It is NOT something that can be accomplished overnight, or even within this decade. Nevertheless, it IS possible to realize the American dream. It IS possible to put our country back on the right track.

We Americans recognize that all is not well, yet we are unsure of who or what to blame. National crises fester without obvious solution; institutions of government and industry consistently fail to act in a constructive fashion; our standard of living and our quality of life are slipping; and we seem no longer confident that we can leave our children a better world.

The issue that matters most is money: in 1991, each of us worked 128 days to pay for government. The forty hour work week doesn't buy what it used to. More of our children continue to live in the family home after becoming adults, not because they want to but because they can't afford not to. Each of these situations is about money.

But what is money? Where does it come from? *Reinventing America* will answer those questions and explore the relationship between money, politics, and our quality of life. Beginning at the beginning, *Reinventing America* defines how value comes from nature, entering our economic and political life through raw materials. Starting with agriculture, the book describes how a structurally balanced economy can and should work, then shows what happens when an economy is out of balance. It quickly becomes obvious that this, in fact, is the disease afflicting America's political/economic system.

Modern politicians and economists tend to focus on parts rather than the whole. Efforts are made to solve the crime problem, the unemployment problem, the environmental problem, or the trade problem. The relationship of all of these problems, one to the other, is rarely the focus of decision makers who are caught up in crisis management and trying to treat the symptoms rather than cure the disease.

The disease—an economic and political system operating out of structural balance—has given rise to all of the symptoms so obvious in today's American society. This disease begins with pride arising from the experiences of each of us living in this American century. We are legitimately proud of the wealth, diversity, stability, and progress which our system of Democratic Capitalism makes possible. But far too often our pride has disposed us to forget the beliefs and values underlying our system.

American self-worth has become a function of externals such as money, possessions, occupation, and status; it is no longer an outgrowth of our character and standards.

We have become "Hollow Men," as described by poet T.S. Eliot, lost in a world defined by our televisions, telephones, fax machines, and automobiles, and isolated from real human contact. If it isn't on television, it isn't real. We care more about Boris Yeltsin or the victims of the latest natural disaster half a world away as seen on the tube than we care for our neighbor's child with a drug problem. We have lost our direction and our moral sense.

There is today an excessive concentration of economic and political power into the hands of a few. In fact, the accepted economic and political goal today has become the further concentration of this power. Those who win at this game have lost sight of an important truth—they have forgotten that our system of Democratic Capitalism depends for its survival on diversity, independent thought, and true freedom. It depends on the ability of America's people to remain economically and politically independent—to make personal decisions about the character and quality of their lives. If the current trend continues, the end result will be no different than it has ever been when the inequitable concentration of economic and political power reaches critical mass: stagnation, depression, and repression. Everyone will lose.

A possible process for solving America's problems is offered in this book. It is first and foremost a personal solution. Each of us contributes to the problems facing our country as a consequence of our beliefs and the actions we take as a result of our beliefs. Thus, the foundation for a solution is for each of us individually to begin living in a manner that contributes to making things a little better every day. In short, we must begin to solve our nation's problems at the most basic level: with ourselves.

This change of lifestyle will require each of us to

reconsider our belief system and analyze every action we take. We start by becoming more self-aware, by considering how our actions relate to our neighbors, our community, and our country. Our relationship to nature and our place in the world will inevitably be defined by this effort. Then, once we have a better idea of who we are and how we connect with the world around us, we will become involved.

Tackling America's problems from the personal level means accepting responsibility for ourselves and conducting our lives as good stewards of ourselves, our community, and the resources we command. The buck stops here.

Everything we do or choose not to do makes a difference: voting, spending, borrowing, cutting corners at work, telling little white lies, not separating the garbage to recycle cans and paper. Each of us creates the world in which we live. Once this notion is accepted, it has far-reaching implications for each of us and the society we create.

Reinventing America explores the ramifications if we were all to accept personal responsibility for our lives as well as the life of our nation. It offers a series of policy suggestions which will cure many of the symptoms contributing to the crises we now face. It also contains a primer on political and social actions which can equip even the novice to effectively make a difference.

I write from experience: everything in this book that I warn readers against doing is conduct which I have personally engaged in more than once. I confess it has taken me ten years to begin to put myself back together and I'm still a long way from perfection! This book was originally conceived as a collection of personal ruminations, and is being offered to you in hopes that you can benefit from my mistakes. Nevertheless, be prepared to make your own uniquely personal mistakes while "Reinventing America."

As you read on, keep in mind the mission of my book: TO BUILD ENLIGHTENED AND SUSTAINABLE COMMUNITIES AND COUNTRIES. This goal dictates first that each individual understand his or her political and economic potential, and second that citizens take command of the political and economic instruments available in modern society. An obvious offshoot is a synergism of people who are both aware of their potential and able to use the instruments at hand to begin to "Reinvent America."

If you agree with the tenets of *Reinventing America*, wonderful! But I would rather conduct a thoughtful dialogue with someone who disagrees with me than receive a reader's blind, unthinking acceptance of this material. I welcome all correspondence, and I hope this book is so thought-provoking that I have trouble answering all those who write. Hopefully you are learning as you read this and you, in turn, can teach me. Be in touch. You will find my address in the back of the book.

Enjoy *Reinventing America*, question all that you read herein, and decide for yourself what you believe. Then, act accordingly.

December, 1991

Reinventing America

PART ONE

THE CURRENT
SITUATION

Rich rules poor, Debtor must wait on creditor.
Proverbs 22:7

Chapter One

Money
Makes the World Go Round!

DEEP THROAT, THE ANONYMOUS source that brought down Richard Nixon, told reporters to "follow the money." That is good advice for all of us. What we are told by elected officials, the media and business people may be a lie. But money itself does not lie — money just is. If we want to know the truth about something, we need to look where the money goes. In the last ten years the United States has gone from being the world's creditor to being the world's largest debtor. So where did the money go?

This is not a book about Reagan or Bush or Congress bashing, although there is plenty to bash them about. This is not about Japan bashing, either, although it is often tempting. The truth is, the President, Congress, and our foreign competitors are just playing by the rules of the game as they understand them.

The rules evolved over the past 50 or 60 years, and what annoys me is how incredibly foolish they are. Even so, we have all bought into them to one degree or another. What are these rules?

1. "I gotta get it now." We live in a culture of instant gratification. When asked, "When do you need this?" we reply, "Yesterday." The can-do attitude of years past has been molded into the right-now attitude of today. As children we get what-

ever we ask for from our parents. As adults we practice the same approach. How many useless things have we all bought in the last year? How many things do we own two of, or three of? Cars, televisions, stereos, sets of china — these things are cluttering up our lives. Do any of us think about what we buy? About how much food we throw away? Our national motto could be, "I want it all and I want it now!"

2. "If I don't have the money, I'll just charge it." How often do we pay for what we buy with credit cards? How often do we pay off the charges on our credit card statements during the same month the charges appear? Not only are we committed to a personal lifestyle based on instant gratification, we compound that error by paying for what we buy using credit. Many Americans own virtually nothing free and clear. Many of us pay for everything in our lives by the month. Do you ever carry cash? Do you feel proud of yourself because you carry a certain brand of credit card or a certain color card? We have bought into the system of borrowing money rather than earning money, and sooner or later we will have to pay the principal as well as the interest.

3. "I'm entitled. I don't have to earn it. It's mine as a matter of right because I'm an American — a citizen of the richest, most powerful nation on earth." Who do you suppose pays for the quality of life we enjoy? I am referring to schools, parks, monuments, museums, highways, and bridges. Every time we use one of these facilities we spend money, although we are seldom charged for it. Even when we do pay a toll or fee, it rarely covers the cost of usage. Are we willing to pay the price of clean air, clean water, and restrictive land use? If we are not willing, who is? Are we willing to pay the price for the next Kuwait? Before saying yes, are you aware that countries other than ours paid for most of the last war?

4. "I don't have to worry about tomorrow or next year — the government (or my company) will take care of me." Our expectations have soared sky high. This is especially evident in the area of social services (Social Security, Medicare, Medicaid, housing programs), pensions, and profit sharing. But we all know there is no free lunch. Billions are spent annually on social programs. Meanwhile, our grown children have been forced to donate more and more of their paychecks so we can receive benefits today. We have mortgaged their future and it is almost certain they will not receive the services they have been promised. This is a shell game, and we are all losing.

5. "Old is bad, new is good." How old is the car you drive? When was the last time you sold a car because it was worn out? Your old stereo probably worked perfectly when you traded it for a CD player. How often do you replace your wardrobe? We live in a disposable society. Much that is good and in working order we dump because of a change in style or fashion.

6. "If it's broke, don't fix it. Throw it away and go get a new one." We have forgotten how to be good stewards. Maintenance is deferred. Care is not exercised. When a tire is punctured, many people buy a new one rather than patch the old. Appliances are routinely discarded when damaged. Part of this is a consequence of planned obsolescence, but much of it is a matter of personal preference.

7. "It's not my job. It's not my fault." When is the last time you heard this, or said it yourself? We try to keep a low profile, we accept only as much responsibility as necessary, and we avoid accountability for errors. Job descriptions, work rules, and contracts are used as excuses to do as little as possible and to blame the other person when anything goes wrong. The ethic is, do not get involved, do not take

chances, and above all, do not expose yourself to the risk of accountability.

8. "I'm already doing too much — more than my share." We are obsessed with getting our full share, but giving back less than our share. We are a selfish society that tends to overpromise and underdeliver. The challenge is to see how little we can get by with doing, while keeping the paychecks coming. Those in management seek to squeeze the last ounce of effort from workers without giving raises, bonuses, or incentives. Our system has become adversarial.

I could go on, but you get the idea by now. These rules represent the epitome of instant gratification, greed, gluttony, and corruption. The rules show arrogance, shortsightedness, and moral decay. The rules are all about money NOW! Tomorrow be damned.

You have heard the joke, "I must have money, I still have checks." Well, the joke is on America, which has been over-indulging itself on a fifty year spending spree. The money ran out somewhere between 1970 and 1980, but we never stopped spending.

Now, foreign interests are bringing home all of those dollars we overspent, and they are buying America. One out of every eight dollars of real property in the United States is owned by a foreigner. The British own more than anyone else, at the moment. Aided by a weak dollar, they are buying companies in virtually every sector of the economy at what amounts to "fire sale prices." Foreign corporations are building plants all over America, employing Americans and focusing on non-union, low wage locales so they spend less on wages than their American competitors. These plants buy many components and raw materials overseas and pay relatively less in taxes than their American-owned competitors. Most of the upper management is also imported.

America is probably still the strongest, richest nation on earth. The rules are only practiced by a minority of Americans (at least let us hope so); nevertheless, follow the money.

For example, our troops, our technology, and our leaders won the recent Persian Gulf war. The Japanese, Germans, Saudi Arabians, and Kuwaitis paid for most of that war, however, and they will derive the most economic benefit from it. Follow the money.

All right, let us follow the money a little farther—it has not all gone to Japan, Western Europe, and the OPEC countries. A great deal of money has changed hands right here. The most complete analysis of where the money has gone is available in *The Politics of Rich and Poor* by Kevin Phillips.

According to Phillips, in America the rich are getting richer (a lot richer) and the poor are getting poorer. If you work for a living, whether you actually produce something tangible or you labor in the service sector, you are financially worse off today than you were yesterday or the day before. That trend has been fairly constant for more than twenty years.

If you invest or live on investments, "clip coupons," play the stocks or commodities markets, and started off with a good chunk of money you have done better. If you manipulate symbols by dealing in the fields of mass entertainment, marketing, or advertising, buy and sell companies, or work in mergers or acquisitions you have done much better. Those that have, have more; those that don't, won't. The extremes of economic condition, both rich and poor, are becoming more extreme.

9

There are more poor people in America than ever before. There are also more homeless, and more "working poor" who bust their tails and still cannot buy a home, put their children through college, or pay for health insurance.

The middle class is slowly losing ground as well. Children will have a harder time than their parents. College graduates are having a hard time finding a job. The traditional family with one wage earner is a thing of the past. Both spouses have to work to get by now — a result of economic pressure, not women's liberation. When we are employed at all, we are often forced to settle for inadequate or second-rate jobs.

Despite all this, there are more millionaires than ever before. Not only millionaires, but billionaires. Sales of luxury items soared throughout the '80s — items such as expensive cars, homes, jewels, artwork, and so on. The rich are now paying less in taxes than at any time since the '30s. The rich keep getting richer and richer, while the classes in American society fall farther and farther apart. The entire economic system is out of balance.

This lack of balance is why there does not seem to be enough money to go around. It is why school teachers are getting laid off, why it is harder to find a good job. Why, if you have a job, you feel less secure.

Our country is on the "wrong track" and the light we think we see at the end of the tunnel is another train barreling toward us, coming the other way on the same track. In a survey conducted by Richard Wirthlin, Ronald Reagan's pollster during the '80s, (and published by the *Washington Post* on July 14, 1991,) 56 percent of those surveyed believe the country is "seriously off on the wrong track." These people are right.

Novelist Doug Copeland in *Generation X* describes the

41 million people born between 1961 and 1971 as those most devastated by the socioeconomic ills now facing us: recession, A.I.D.S., homelessness, crack, the deficit. He writes that this generation is being forced to get a "McJob: a low-pay, low-prestige, low-dignity, low-benefit, no-future job in the service sector. Frequently considered a satisfying career choice by people who have never held one." We are turning into a service economy as more and more manufacturing jobs are shipped overseas.

Regarding children, Senator Mark Hatfield, in the *Congressional Record*, reported that, "One American child in five now lives in poverty; another one in five lives with a single parent. By the year 2000, both numbers will be one in four if current trends continue." He went on to list other statistics: 135,000 children carry a gun to school each day; every 32 seconds a teenaged woman becomes pregnant; every 55 seconds a child is born whose mother does not hold even a high school diploma; and every 14 hours a child aged five or younger is murdered.

Industry is a mess as well. Kevin Kearns, a fellow at the Economic Strategy Institute, reports that U.S. automakers lost 4.7 billion dollars during the first two quarters of 1991. He says that Japanese import sales now exceed 30 percent of the U.S. auto market, up almost 300 percent for them since 1978. The Japanese continue to move ahead despite an overhaul of American factories, which now create better quality autos, show higher worker productivity, and are better managed than ever before.

In his column of September 1, 1991, George Will described a troubling trend. As the American economy stumbled into recession, the very people we depend upon to manage companies, protect jobs, and restore corporate growth—the CEOs of our leading corporations—were cashing in on their companies at an unprecedented rate. Will wrote, "The compensation of CEOs is generally disproportionate and often ludicrous in light of corporate performance." For example, even though corporate profits fell seven percent in 1990, pay to CEOs went up seven percent. The American CEO "earns" between 85 and 100 times what an average worker earns. That level of compensation may sound reasonable until you compare it to the ratio of CEO/worker compensation in other countries. In Japan, the ratio is 17 to 1, in France and Germany about 25 to 1, and in Britain 35 to 1. The obvious effect of this American excess is to focus the CEO toward his or her self-interest at the exclusion of all else. There appears to be no relation between performance and compensation in many American companies — they are being looted by management as they struggle through a recession. The losers are those of us who work for, rely on stock dividends for income, or otherwise depend upon these companies. While these CEOs are getting richer, what is happening to the rest of us whose jobs are at stake?

Regarding education, columnist Richard Cohen in a recent editorial wrote, "Washington, D.C., first in murder and probably in monuments, is first in something else as well: self-delusion. Students here who took the recent national math test were ranked next to last in skills but first in responding to the statement, 'I am good at mathematics.' This paradox produces a dilemma: you don't know whether to laugh or cry."

Another laugh or cry situation was reported June 19, 1991, with a *Washington Post* headline, "Luxurious Fairfax Government Center Readied Amid Austerity." The accompanying article described the new 100 million dollar complex, which features a $35,000 granite conference table, a fitness center, and private elevators for elected officials. These few examples of recent press coverage of current events and issues represent disturbing trends.

Multiple crises have shaken our American self-confidence and threaten our lifestyle. Decision makers appear unable to assign priorities, balance competing interests, or accept responsibility for the decisions they have made. The result is paralysis. There appears to be no single reason for this stasis; multiple factors have brought us to this point:

Major political parties are in hock to so many interests, they are structurally unable to offer real solutions.

The short-term priority of winning the next election is the only priority for most elected officials and short term profit drives business decision making.

Interest groups take more and more extreme positions in order to attract sufficient dollars to stay alive. They practice confrontation rather than compromise because that sells better in the next fund raising letter.

Society is evolving into groups of polarized activists who use the threat of losing an election to exert pressure on political officeholders. This "dialogue" between activists and politicians is ignored by the mass of cynical, disengaged citizens who have no time, money, or energy to waste on such politics. The officeholders' natural tendency, motivated by fear of electoral defeat, is to offend no one. Consequently, decisions do not get made, substance gives way to form, and our country suffers.

The actual business of government is left in the hands of a professional elite, the "fourth branch" employed by government to provide the services expected by taxpayers. These professionals are too often more concerned with paychecks, turf, status, job security, retirement benefits, and finding a high-paying job after leaving government than

13

they are with serving the public. These are the bureaucrats who remain in government year after year, regardless of what party controls the White House or Congress. They write regulations and enforce them, maintain an immunity to accountability, and become increasingly arrogant and independent with each passing year.

Government is therefore less and less responsive to the needs of people, and more and more driven to act for its own convenience and self-interest. Quite simply, those in government are desperate to preserve the status quo. The easy decision is the one that gets made. Balance the budget? Why bother, when the country can borrow more money and tax its citizens more?

The bureaucracy known as government never gets smaller. Burgeoning numbers of people directly or indirectly depend on the government for their daily bread, while fewer people actually produce wealth or value. "Tax Freedom Day" is the day that marks the point in the year when you and I can finally work for our own benefit because we have earned enough money to pay our taxes for the year. It used to occur in February; now it arrives in May. Each of us had to work 128 days in 1991 to pay for government. Was it worth it?

Ronald Reagan once asked, before his election as President and before he created (with the advice and consent of the Democrats in Congress) the largest budget deficit in history, "Are you better off now than you were four years ago?" The answer is still no, and the trends indicate that our situation continues to deteriorate.

Government must be held to the same standards of responsiveness as the business sector. Our government must become market driven. From top to bottom, government must serve its constituents, not the other way around. By applying common sense, we can change government, making it profitable to its citizens. More important, we can convince government to leave us alone, or at the very least, keep it from making our lives any more miserable.

Our leaders tell us the economy is starting to recover and that the recession was really not so severe. Our leaders wave the flag, march the troops, and set off the fireworks. And most of them will probably be reelected. But, if you follow the money, you can recognize the lie. Follow the money and you understand the danger.

Our problems are not only governmental, however. Business appears less competitive, the environment is hurting, families are threatened, kids are not being educated, and we seem to be paying more for everything while enjoying it all less. Many of us sense that the whole situation may be getting out of hand. We, as Americans, are losing our confidence and our self-esteem. More and more of us are giving up, beginning to think it's OK to "go along to get along." We cheat on our taxes, our jobs, and our spouses, and we cut corners every day in everything we do. We have put ourselves in danger of being defeated as a people, losing our humanity and dooming ourselves to lives of despair.

The solutions necessary to recapture government and put it to work as a positive force for all of us will not be implemented unless we first take control of our own lives. We must put our family house in order, and then once we are in control of our private lives, we can take these same actions to put business, education, and other social institutions back on track. We all criticize government and other large institutions, but we should remember that those organizations are really only a reflection of ourselves. The place to begin the battle to reinvent America is within our minds. After we

15

have rededicated ourselves to the "American Ideal," we can enlist family, friends, neighbors, and co-workers to make those ideals reality once again.

To achieve these objectives, we must assume responsibility for ourselves and assert our rights. We must remind ourselves of an often-forgotten founding principle upon which this Representative Democracy has been built: All power not specifically delegated is reserved to the people and their representatives. We must accept responsibility for our lives, act in our own enlightened self-interest, and not give government or any other large institution the power to do our thinking for us.

If we succeed, we shall define a code of ethics which will naturally flow from the way we live day to day; we will live with integrity, responsibility, and commitment. In this way we will have dealt with the underlying causes, not just the blatant symptoms, of our current confusion.

The analysis you are reading looks at two root causes of America's problems. The first is political paralysis; most people understand the nature of this paralysis, even if they are unable to agree on how to solve it. Second, our economy is out of balance, but most people do not understand either the reasons for it, or the solutions.

Part One of this book, "The Current Situation," attempts to explain the reality of our basic economic imbalance here in the United States.

Part Two, "Government & Politics," defines the nature, theory, and reality of government and politics upon which the United States of America is based and how political paralysis can progress.

Part Three, "Holistic Politics," defines a new way of looking at government and politics, and presents a series of policy recommendations for dealing with many of the issues threatening the wellbeing of this country and us, its citizens.

Part Four, "Reinventing America," offers a personal plan that you can apply to help begin reinventing our country. It is a course of action to treat the political and economic paralysis smothering us, and to put us back on the right track before we have a wreck.

Americans have written a lot of checks for a lot of years. Now those checks are starting to hit the bank, but there are not enough funds to pay them all. It is time to pay the piper. But how do we pay? How did it all happen?

Chapter Two

The Value of Money

HOW DO WE KNOW WHAT OUR money is worth? What is money anyway? This does not concern how the Congress or the Federal Reserve define money. What we are concerned about is money as it relates to personal experience.

The answer was first defined in the 1700s by Adam Smith in his book, *The Wealth of Nations*. To paraphrase and update Smith, you are rich or poor depending on how many conveniences and amusements you can enjoy in life. This focuses into how much labor you can command or afford to purchase: if you can afford to pay a chef to cook your dinner and a waitperson to serve it you are richer than the person who can only afford a fast-food meal, who is richer in turn than the person who must buy groceries and cook for him or herself. In this manner, according to Smith, labor becomes the "real measure of the exchangeable value of all commodities."

Smith defines the real price of an item as "the toil and trouble of acquiring it." Under his theory, you know what your money is worth on the basis of what it "costs" you to get it and what the money can get you when you spend it. Of course we can get money by borrowing it, or it can be given to us as a gift, but most of us cannot survive long relying on borrowed or birthday dollars. You must earn money, then spend no more than you earn. This is a principle as true for the nation as it is for you and I in our daily lives. Unfortunately, our nation has yet to learn its lesson.

Setting aside gifts and loans and focusing on earned money (wages, profits, interest, rents, etc.), it is possible to define a relationship between what you do to earn money and how much you earn. After that, you can determine what your earned money will buy, and thus evolve some mental equations to determine the value of your money in your life. In this sense, the value of money for each of us is the relationship between what we do to earn our money and what that money will eventually buy us. This is the bottom line of what Adam Smith was saying.

Millions of people are engaged in the same pursuits as you and I: earning money and spending money. Together we become and create an "economy." Economists, those people who study relationships between earning and spending, are fond of trying to "manage" the economy, but their efforts usually unbalance the economy instead, resulting in frequent recessions and an occasional depression.

Digging a little deeper, the value underlying what we do that inspires someone to pay us to do it must come from somewhere. But where? What creates value?

ALL VALUE COMES FROM NATURE.

Nature gives us value in the form of raw materials and, as a part of nature, people add to that value by changing those raw materials into various finished products that can be used or consumed. By raw materials, I refer to agricultural produce, timber, fish, and minerals. We contribute the final "raw material" ingredient — labor. These things, each provided naturally, are the source of all value.

In prehistoric and moving into historic times, all value

was created and consumed in the effort to survive. People gathered nuts and berries and hunted wild game, then ate what they had killed or collected. Eventually, agriculture developed. As agricultural efficiency increased, food surpluses consistently accumulated. Not having to worry every waking moment about food led to more complex societies based on a division of labor. As society became more complex there arose a need to quantify and keep track of values being exchanged between people. For that reason, a market economy using money was created.

The value of the money in days past was a function of the raw materials grown upon or extracted from the land, in relationship to the goods and services provided to the growers and extractors by people who were not actually involved in the growing or extracting. Put in other words, assessing the value of money as it related to these raw materials became a function of the labor necessary to create and to market the raw materials. This is what Adam Smith described in *The Wealth of Nations*.

Is there a correct, quantifiable, unchanging relationship between the value of the raw materials provided by nature and the total labor, goods, and services in society? Assuming there is, how can the correct relationship be discovered and the correct value be assigned to money?

As in all aspects of nature, there exists a natural balance between the raw materials produced, their value (hence the value of money), and the total output of society. This natural balance can be discovered by study, research, trial and error.

In Book One, Chapter Seven of *The Wealth of Nations*, Adam Smith identifies a "natural" and "market" price of commodities. (See Appendix A for Smith's actual words on the subject.) Smith refers to the natural price of a commodity as being neither more nor less than the expenses of the

20

raw material and the labor to reap it, combined with an ordinary rate of profit. The market price of a commodity is the actual price at which it is sold, which may be above, below, or exactly the same as its natural price.

Market price is regulated by supply and demand; the quantity of any commodity at market conforms to the demand for it. The natural price is the "central" price, or the price toward which a commodity continually gravitates.

Obviously, market prices could continuously exceed natural prices, but seldom could they fall below, or the producer would feel the loss and adjust accordingly to bring them up to the natural level. To quote Smith, "This at least would be the case where there was perfect liberty."

George Peek, author of *Equality for Agriculture* called this natural balance "fair exchange value," a phrase he coined shortly after World War I. Peek believed that when the total economy operates in balance, the total income earned in the economy must be seven times the money earned in the raw material sector. When this ratio is maintained, all sectors of the economy will function in a financially solvent and prosperous balance.

When an economy is out of balance, the income required for its operation does not dramatically decrease, but the money to provide that income becomes scarce. The shortfall is made up by debt or inflation of the money supply, or a combination of the two. The longer the economy stays out of balance the worse the effect. Eventually there is a collapse, resulting in a breakdown of the economy and sometimes of the government itself. Eventually the laws outlined by Adam Smith in *The Wealth of Nations* must be obeyed. Those natural balances can be postponed and the effects of deviation from the natural price can be hidden for awhile, but eventually the piper must be paid.

21

To really understand Peek's "fair exchange value" equation or Adam Smith's "natural and market price of commodities," consider an example: nature provides a raw material such as wheat, oil, fish, or a tree, and someone works to harvest, pump, catch, or cut the raw material — labor. We will focus here on wheat.

Adam Smith stated, "It is the work of nature which remains after inducting or compensating everything which can be regarded as the work of man." He believed that agriculture puts into motion a greater succession of productive labor than does manufacturing, for the farmer starts not merely with the raw material (wheat), but with the means to create that raw material (nature itself), which he directs with his own labor into producing the most profitable plants. Within this scheme, wheat appears at the bottom of the value chain.

If we accept Peek's "fair exchange value" ratio of seven, then every dollar of value created in agriculture and raw materials, in this case wheat, will result in seven dollars of value being generated throughout the economy. Why, though, should we rely on the ratio of one dollar of raw materials income to seven of total earned income in the economy?

In 1942, based in large part on the work of the Raw Materials National Council, the United States adopted the War Stabilization Act with a provision known as the Steagall Amendment. The Steagall Amendment incorporated the one to seven ratio. A 1967 interview with Carl H. Wilken, one of the leaders of the Raw Materials National Council from that period, was recounted by writer Charles Walters in his book, *Unforgiven*, and reveals the reasoning behind the one to seven ratio. This interview is reprinted in Appendix B.

According to Wilken, national income is nothing more than raw material income times five or farm income times seven, which he referred to as a trade turn. The ratio is based on efficiency: in 1787, nine of ten people were farmers, but by 1850 that changed to five out of ten. The trade turn moved up to two, in that one farmer was required to feed two people. By the time of World War I, the turn came to five when computed in terms of all raw materials, and seven when compared to farm income, meaning that one farmer could feed seven people.

As evidence of this ratio, Wilken cited several types of statistics. He said that gross farm income fell 6.8 billion dollars between 1929 and 1933, and national income fell 47.6 billion dollars — exactly seven dollars of national income was lost for every farm dollar lost. From 1940 to 1943, gross farm income increased to 23.4 billion dollars, and national income went up about seven times to 170.3 billion dollars, a feat ending the Depression which was accomplished so quickly because of World War II. In 1945, the trade turn again proved to be 7.01, while over the years spanning 1928 to 1953, it averaged 7.04.

Wilken went on to assert that agriculture continues to turn out an earned income on the ratio of seven, but this amount is now only about half that required to operate our economy. The rest is unearned income developed by injecting borrowed money into the economy.

Asked to clarify the notion of unearned income, or income generated by debt, Wilken called it capital debt — debt which is used as if it were capital funds. "An economy can only expand its production facilities, or its capital investment, out of profit," he said. "It cannot borrow capital beyond its ability to generate profits to pay it off." Debt itself is not inherently bad; only when the amount of debt exceeds the ability to retire it, as when debt functions as capital, do problems arise.

On a national level, every dollar of this capital debt which is being used as if it were profit generates five dollars of national income. This sounds reasonable until statistics are analyzed: it takes about $5.50 of this national income to generate just one dollar of profit with which to retire that debt or even pay the interest on it. In other words, the economy falls behind more each day, until the debt can no longer be paid back, nor can it be forgiven. Our country faces this problem right now.

Worded differently, Wilken said that, as of 1967, "for every dollar income you've increased in the last six years, you've added two dollars to your debt." Try to walk up a hill taking one step forward and two backwards. Since 1967, at the time this interview was conducted, the "backwards" trend has accelerated.

When the interviewer cited economists who argue that it does not matter, we owe the money to ourselves, Wilken said, "That's the trouble....that's 50 billion dollars of interest that has to be paid on one trillion dollars [of debt added from 1950 to 1967]. Now you have a 20 percent operating profit for the United States as a whole, so it takes well over five dollars of national income to generate one dollar of profit to pay that interest. We may owe it to ourselves, but ourselves is really a few millionaires."

In essence, what Wilken was describing in the interview is a geometrical progression: on the basis of interest alone, at the rate of 7 per cent, debt doubles in a decade. This figure is lower than interest rates experienced in this country over the past twenty years. Now go back to the example of wheat.

Wheat is sold by the farmer for four dollars a bushel.

By the time that bushel of wheat is fully consumed and all the effects of growing, harvesting, processing, selling, etc., are finished, a total of $28 of revenue will have been generated, based on Peek's "fair exchange value."

This money does not go just to the farmer. It is divided up among people throughout society. People who sell seed or fertilizer to the farmer get a piece of the action. People who provide equipment ranging from shareholders in the manufacturing company, to managers, employees, distributors, dealers, and salespeople in the showroom also get some of the $28. A portion of the income will go to the farmer's family doctor, lawyer, banker, and minister. The utility and phone company get their share of the income, as do the various levels of government who tax all of these people. As the wheat moves through the system, everyone from truck drivers to bakers to grocery store operators get part of the income that results from the value generated by that wheat and the labor the farmer invested in its production. If the economy is in balance and operating in harmony with Peek's principle of "fair exchange value," all prosper. On the other hand, if the market price remains for long below the natural prices defined by Smith, disaster will result.

Consider how the economy functions when it is out of balance. Assume the farmer sold the wheat for $3 a bushel even though it cost $3.75 in out-of-pocket expenses and another 25 cents for his or her labor and profit to grow and harvest the bushel; in other words, true costs add up to $4. The total income generated in the economy from that bushel will still be seven times what the farmer received or $21. The farmer will have lost 75 cents in out-of-pocket expenses on the bushel and received no compensation or profit for the labor invested to grow and harvest the wheat. But this is only the beginning of the problems, because the farmer should have received $4 for his wheat, which would have generated $28 for the economy. By underselling, the economy has been denied $7.

Society as a whole will not just stop spending money. People will go on with their lives, or at least try to continue on as before, but there will be cutbacks because Smith's law of supply and demand will operate. If the price of wheat is controlled by the government (and it is, by the way) the farmer and all those who depend on the farmer for their income and their food will begin to protest the underpricing of the wheat.

The political system will react by trying to mitigate the damage resulting from a market price for wheat which has been set artificially below the natural price, as specified by Smith's and Peek's principles. Loan programs, crop subsidies, artificial price supports, and the rest will be implemented to cushion the negative impact on the farmer and all the other people in society.

These people will be reluctant to change their lifestyles, nor is that made absolutely necessary, because government subsidies will artificially reduce the level of change required to react to the market. Peek's "fair exchange value" and Smith's law of supply and demand will be violated, with eventual catastrophic results.

First, people will tend to borrow money to make up the shortfall in earned income throughout the economy. Starting with the farmer, assume for the sake of argument that government programs loan the farmer 65 cents a bushel and that the farmer finds a way to cut expenses by 35 cents a bushel. This enables the farmer to "get by" selling the bushel of wheat for $3 and borrowing the difference needed for expenses and an income. Of course the deferred expenses of 35 cents a bushel the farmer cut back on his or her business may actually end up raising the out-of-pocket expenses (the farmer might have to buy a new engine after failing to buy antifreeze — guessing wrong on the weather could backfire in the effort to save a little bit of money). One way or another, the farmer finds a way to "get by."

With the rule of one to seven, total borrowings in society will be about seven times what the farmer borrowed. This means that debt related to this bushel of wheat will be seven times the 65 cents per bushel borrowed by the farmer, or \$4.55 throughout society. This debt will take many forms. The lawyer will charge lunch on a credit card rather than paying cash. The baker will get paid by the supermarket chain 90 days after the bread is sold instead of within 30 days. The government will borrow money (maybe from Social Security Trust Funds, maybe from the Japanese) to pay unemployment benefits. People who are laid off in the inevitable cutbacks will delay payment on their utility bills, or maybe just skip town. Other people will forego paying for inessential services (at least services they consider inessential) like health insurance.

The same ratio will apply with respect to the 35 cents per bushel that the farmer stops spending. Throughout society an amount equal to seven times that, or \$2.45, will be cut back. Consequently, infrastructure may be allowed to deteriorate, maintenance will probably be deferred, and marginal employees will be temporarily laid off or entirely terminated.

Unfortunately, the effect of the policies described in the forgoing example can easily be seen in the pervasive decline of our society's economic health as predicted by the theories of Smith and Peek. It is very close to the reality we have lived over the last 50 years in these United States.

The workings of this economic system have been the

subject of much confusion over the years. Smith's position has been distorted to describe a world of cutthroat competition and capitalistic exploitation, when his writings really attempted to define an interdependent, cooperative effort by all members of society that is guided by the invisible hand of the free market.

Many farmers today have developed a concept known as parity which essentially mirrors Peek's "fair exchange value" concept and is based on natural pricing. Parity, unfortunately, has also been aligned in a popular sense with the idea of social justice for farmers. In this sense, the definition of parity has been twisted to refer to a pricing mechanism reliant upon welfare assistance to ensure farmers a fair living.

In his book *The Farm Fiasco*, James Bovard rightfully attacks both the notion and the practice of parity as it refers to social welfare for the farmer. Nevertheless, he proceeds to confuse the issue by expanding his attack to include examples of parity as it relates to natural price or "fair exchange value." Bovard does not correctly differentiate between the two usages of parity, a habit common in governmental and economic circles which has caused a great deal of confusion for the American public. As used here, parity refers only to Peek's principle of "fair exchange value" which emerges from Adam Smith's concept of natural price.

It is a mistake to adopt the other definition of parity, that of a moral pricing system to assure equitable distribution of income, even though farmers and their opponents at the United States Department of Agriculture (USDA) and Congress have done so. Their mistake results from years of compounded misjudgements beginning in 1948, when prices of raw materials and particularly agricultural commodities were first held below the natural price, as Adam Smith conceived it. To cushion the impact of this strategy, various subsidy programs, loan programs, and thinly-disguised welfare programs were designed and implemented by the USDA. Farmers began to realize that survival depended on "playing the game." Those who played well received their price supports, low interest loans, and trade barriers. Their rallying cry was, and is, "parity." Those who played poorly, or who did not realize what game they were in, saw their farms auctioned off.

The parity game, with moves like limiting sugar imports or supporting milk prices, makes the USDA's approach to agriculture appear more consistent with an economy envisioned by Karl Marx than one operating by the invisible hand of Adam Smith's market economy.

The current public policy arguments, in which parity encourages artificial price supports or subsidies to struggling farmers, can only be understood when the financial underpinnings of agriculture are understood. Today's financial system is designed to maintain raw materials market prices at levels below their natural prices. Occasionally, a trade association representing a specific group of producers, such as dairy farmers, wins a battle to obtain partial relief from the dampening effect of this system. However, the mass of farm products and other raw materials are continually sold for less than it costs to produce them.

Adam Smith was correct when he pointed out that where the system operates in "perfect liberty," people receiving market prices for their goods that are lower than the natural prices for those goods will recognize their losses and take steps to end them. The effect of government policy has been to constrain the system, until it operates without perfect liberty:

1. The policy of cheap food leaves American farmers to

compete with foreign producers even while they face unreasonable disadvantages in doing so.

2. However, when production costs exceed market price,
and produce or products are sold at less than their natural
prices, government mitigates the inevitable negative economic impact by welfare assistance, price supports, and
other favorable exceptions. These actions essentially "buy
off" or silence the more politically important and powerful
raw materials producers and farmers insulating those companies and farmers from market reality.

3. At the same time, raw materials and produce needed
by developing countries for their local consumption and
economic development are needlessly diverted to the United
States, resulting in even larger surpluses here and scarcity
overseas.

4. Economic and political dislocation here and abroad
is the result. This dislocation manifests as food shortages
and famine in developing countries who must sell their local
produce abroad to generate hard currency; at the same time
America pays dearly to store its own surplus foods. Dislocation also manifests as massive migration from rural to
urban environments throughout the world, which strains
infrastructure to the breaking point, and as the increased
debt seen in all countries and all sectors of each economy.

5. The lack of adequate earned income caused by
holding raw materials and farm products at levels below the
American natural price has caused a worsening shortage of
money in the economy. This imbalance has been artificially
corrected by injecting debt into the economy to replace
earned income and to enable government to finance massive
subsidies, welfare, and entitlements. The cost of the welfare
programs necessary to prevent total destruction of our
economy's raw materials sector and to replace earned in-

come throughout the economy with debt becomes a significant burden on the American public, leading to higher taxes, deficit spending, and increasing levels of individual and corporate debt.

6. Finally, all of the dollars spent to import raw materials and consumer goods create a significant American trade deficit and ever-increasing loan obligations to foreign governments, banks, and investors.

It should be clear by now that the policy must be corrected, or the system will collapse. If you are skeptical of this analysis, take a look at the successful and unsuccessful economies operating in our world today. Where agriculture and raw materials have been abused, such as in the former U.S.S.R., the economy is in disrepair. Where they have been protected, such as in Western Europe and Japan, economies are sturdy.

What is really happening today in the United States of America?

According to the United States Department of Agriculture (USDA) it currently (Feb. 1991) costs an American farmer $4.14 to grow a bushel of wheat. That bushel could only be sold for about three dollars. According to Charles Walters, publisher of the magazine, *Acres, U.S.A.*, the actual "fair exchange value" as defined by Peek's system, or the natural price for a bushel of wheat as defined by Adam Smith, is about ten dollars. Wheat is the example here, but it is not an exception. These same lopsided prices apply, or have applied, for most of the last 30 to 40 years in all sectors that produce raw materials in our economy.

This means that the federal government is, and has been, spending billions of dollars on relief for farmers, forest product companies, mining companies, oil companies, and the like for dozens of years. Additional billions are

31

loaned to farmers each year, then more billions from subsidies and incentive programs go to pay farmers not to grow their crops. Agriculture is the example here, but I am not trying to discriminate. Our entire economy is out of whack for these same reasons. Consider the oil depletion allowance, favorable treatment of timber companies harvesting national forests, and mining companies using public lands. These subsidies, coupled with free trade policies that force Americans to play on an uneven field against foreign competitors, are the first in a series of dominoes falling throughout the American economy that will eventually lead to calamity.

In *The Politics of Rich and Poor*, Kevin Phillips reports that at year-end 1980, foreigners owed us about 150 billion dollars more than we owed them. By year-end 1987, the balance had reversed: we owed foreigners about 400 billion dollars more than they owed us. In exact numbers, we experienced a negative plunge of 532.5 billion dollars in just seven years. Comparing our performance with other nations of the world during that same period, Japan went from a positive position of being owed 30 billion dollars to an even better positive position of 230 billion; Germany started at a positive position of 40 billion dollars and ended up at positive 170 billion; and Britain shifted from a 45 billion dollar positive balance to a 175 billion dollar positive balance in net external assets.

The results are painfully obvious. Sure, the Savings and Loan crisis, the trade deficit, and the unemployment rate get lots of press. But, those are just numbers. They are merely symptoms of the underlying problem. If you have tried to borrow money lately you can feel the difference. Our children will have a much tougher time than we did as they try to make a living. Just finding a job is getting harder.

I am not talking about a "McJob" in a fast food joint, I mean a real job with enough money to raise a family and buy a home and send the kids to college.

Problems are not over for those of us currently employed, either. Quoting Kevin Phillips, "For all workers, white-collar as well as blue-collar, their real average weekly wage — calculated at constant 1977 dollars — fell from $191.41 a week in 1972 to $171.07 in 1986."

That is why it seems hard to make ends meet. Now, both spouses working is not a luxury and is not optional.

During the early 1980s the trends of the last 50 years culminated in a farm crisis, the scrapping of most of our fishing industry, and crises in the mining and timber industries. The ripple or domino effect of this violation of the concept of "fair exchange value" led to crises in automotive, financial, and housing sectors of the economy. Now government in the early '90s is facing an incredible financial mess.

The crisis is so bad that George Bush was forced to retreat from his "no new taxes" pledge almost two years before seeking re-election — something we all know he was not anxious to do. Luckily, he appears to have been saved by Saddam Hussein and a successful war financed by Japan, Western Europe, and the Kingdoms of the Middle East. Nevertheless, the underlying structural problems show no signs of going away. In fact, the Congressional Research Service predicts that United States domestic and international indebtedness combined will double between 1987 and 1991, and double again by 1995. A final note of cheer, the government announced on July 16, 1991, that the 1992 budget deficit will be an all time record of 348 billion dollars.

33

Chapter Three

What Went Wrong?

WHAT ARE THE ROOTS OF THE DECAY and neglect which surround us? What went wrong with our country?

We can use money to understand what is happening in American politics and business. Money, when we consider it in the context of what Adam Smith or George Peek had to say, enables us to see more clearly that our country got onto the wrong track some time back.

Digging toward the roots of our problems, I think they began when the collective consciousness of America started to focus on wealth and power as ends in themselves. Americans began to believe that money was more than a thing; it came to be regarded as a "good thing," as an end rather than a means to an end. People with money are "good," people without money are somehow morally deficient or "bad," and the culture of money came into being.

In his book, *The Spirit of Democratic Capitalism*, Michael Novak pointed out that what sets the American experience apart is not just the ability to accumulate wealth. Rather, it is the political freedom embodied in the Constitution and the Bill of Rights in conjunction with the economic freedom of the capitalistic system. Both are necessary components.

With these freedoms comes responsibility. It is necessary that Americans serve a dual function: not only are we economic and political actors, we must also act as conservators of the political system, our natural resources, and the economy.

We receive the political and economic system from preceding generations, we serve as stewards of that system for our allotted time, and then we pass it on to the next generation. If we have done a good job, we will have conserved the principal — our country's assets — and added to it. If we have done a good job, we will pass along more to the next generation than we received, even while living well ourselves.

That at least is the theory. The reality, for at least the last 50 years, has been quite different. We have become a nation of spendthrifts. We have spent the interest generated by our assets, contributed little, and nearly looted the principal as well. I wish I could say you instead of we, but I am as guilty as everyone else of these acts.

We are the problem.

Specifically, we as a nation came out of the experience of the second World War with a fat head. Pax Americana became a reality. This was the culmination of a trend that had started with the concept of Manifest Destiny over a century earlier. The American Empire spread across the continent. Then, our superior political and economic systems brought us to a point of political and economic domination of the world. This was not necessarily bad, in and of itself. What was bad was our impulse to take ourselves too seriously and to believe our own PR.

We became arrogant. We began to take our position for granted, and began to consider our preeminence in the world as a "right." As citizens of the number one nation, we began to expect and demand ever more entitlements. As workers we began to coast a little, and work less efficiently. As managers

35

we substituted macho pride for hard work and sound thinking.

While we as a nation gloated, others worked their behinds off. While we opened our borders in an unlimited, ill-considered free trade policy, others protected their raw materials sector and basic industries. While we forgot about the concept of "fair exchange value," others did not. We spent and consumed, while others saved. We lost our natural balance, and we set off down the wrong track.

I am not talking here about government, business, or education, although each of these groups participated in the foolishness with gusto. I am talking about each of us individually and personally. Our thoughts and actions are what is relevant.

Each of us who participated in a culture of conspicuous consumption, without producing at a level to sustain that consumption, is a part of the problem. With each passing year, more thousands of Americans have joined the ranks of the 19th century buffalo hunters who slaughtered millions of animals, took the hides, and left the meat to rot. We have descended on the continent like a plague of locusts, leaving piles of trash, dirty air, discarded cars, and fast food joints as evidence of our passing. The quick buck, the fast hustle, and the leisure ethic have replaced hard work, responsibility, and "pay as you go" in our credo.

This is not a condemnation of luxury, leisure, or fine living. This is a condemnation of unearned luxury, unearned leisure, and unearned fine living. Specifically, this is a condemnation of a system composed of the following kinds of senseless things:

An income tax that takes more from people who produce more, creating disincentives to produce, and simultaneously creates incentives to spend rather than to save or conserve.

Two unequal yet parallel retirement programs — one the familiar "civilian" Social Security program, the other accomodating several million government workers by offering them better benefits, after less time served, which have been subsidized by the "civilian" taxpayers.

A civil service system that makes it virtually impossible to fire a government worker regardless of how lazy and incompetent he or she may be.

An Administrative Procedures Act that lets bureaucrats at whim issue regulations which have the force of law but for which the issuer cannot be held accountable.

A medical system that costs more than any other in the world, yet denies access to 37 million Americans.

A criminal justice system in which we are willing to spend $40,000 per prisoner per year to lock up more people per capita than either the Soviets or the South Africans.

An educational system which pays teachers so poorly they can no longer afford to teach.

A drug policy which artificially maintains scarcity, inflating the price of drugs and making it possible to become rich by pushing drugs. A side effect of this drug policy is to set the government and its citizens at odds with each other.

These are some of the results of the underlying moral, ethical, and spiritual crises we face. As a result of these crises, we have failed both individually and as a nation to adhere to a sound fiscal/economic policy based upon the natural balance of "fair exchange value." Once the underpinnings of a balanced economic system are knocked away, all other relationships are called into question.

The resulting economic pressure forces individual, corporate, and governmental decision makers to become short-sighted and selfish, acting against the long term self-interest in each of these areas. Confidence is lost, long term considerations go out the window, and the focus is on survival. The rule becomes "look out for number one" at all costs. The attitude toward our neighbors, co-workers, customers, and employers becomes one of suspicion and fear. Each of us tends to become more likely to see the "bad" or "different" aspects of our neighbor. Our neighbor becomes less of a person and more of an object. We tend to transfer our fears and animosity toward these neighbors by assuming they seek to take advantage of us and expecting the worst from them. This becomes justification for a preemptory first strike, which we justify to ourselves on the basis that "it's a dog-eat-dog world."

We have become a nation of strangers. We are alone in our strange land, rootless wanderers moving from city to city, job to job, marriage to marriage. In *A Different Drummer*, M. Scott Peck defines this as a loss of our sense of community. We are no longer as likely to consider ourselves members of the American community, much less members of a community defined in terms of state, city, church, school, profession, or neighborhood. Now, we are more likely to define ourselves in terms of what we own, or what we drive, or the house we live in. We don't "see" the poor or the homeless or the junkie, much less feel benevolent or compassionate toward these people. "They" have become different than "us." "They" are part of the problem. "They" need to get out of our way.

There are four main reasons for our loss of community. First is the arrogance, discussed above, which overtook the United States following our victories of World War II. That arrogance is a two-edged sword; it is not only the root cause of political and economic dissipation in America, it also contributes to our loss of community. Prior to 1940, such arrogance would have been overcome by the on-going, vital political dialogue that occurred in thousands of coffee shops, barber shops, churches, political clubs, and front porches. That kind of political dialogue has all but ceased to exist today.

Gone are the hundreds of thousands of independent thinkers who interacted with other independent thinkers, striving to develop their understanding of the issues. Now, we have a few hundred "thinkers" whose place behind the podium is determined by their popularity ratings. Their extreme positions, provocative talk, and pandering to the baser emotions have replaced thoughtful consideration, compromise, and community. What is wrong is that political and economic dialogue in the United States is dominated by radio and TV talk shows and the words of a few dozen nationally syndicated writers.

We are becoming homogenized — losing needed diversity in our points of view. There is not a dime's worth of difference between the national leadership of the Democratic and Republican parties. George Bush, paragon of the Republican party, and Robert Strauss, former head of the Democrats, have more in common with each other than they do with the rank and file of their respective parties. They are so in tune that as of this writing, Strauss works for George Bush as our new ambassador to Russia.

Without a sense of community where we can maintain strong personal relationships with friends, neighbors, and co-workers, it becomes difficult to tolerate divergent opinions. We simply do not trust each other enough to accept differences, without making judgements about the personal worth of the individual with whom we disagree.

Although arrogance started us on this road to doom, we would not have gone as far as we have but for three other more quantifiable and concrete factors. They are automo-

39

biles, television, and institutional growth, and all three have contributed to the destruction of our sense of community.

None of these is inherently "bad." Automakers are not a horde of Nazis building concentration camps, nor are television executives disciples of Orwell who try to destroy originality and independent thought. The heads of large organizations do not intentionally seek to stifle individuality or creativity in their workforce. Nevertheless, the auto has contributed to a process that has turned central cities into wastelands. Television has limited diversity and independence, while contributing to our confusion regarding what is real in our society. And large organizations have too often contributed to the isolation of the individual.

Chances are you, like I, live in a suburb several miles from where you work. If you are married, your spouse probably works also, and his or her job will be several miles from yours. The children attend school at yet another distant location. We are hard pressed to live in today's world without at least one car, probably two. Our homes are designed to include parking for a car or cars. No one walks. In general, to go where we need to go, we spend from 15 minutes (if lucky) to over an hour (in most cases) alone in the car. Vast networks of streets, collectors, parkways, and freeways have been built to enable us to drive to work, then home again. Acres of city land have been razed to build parking garages. During the day, major workplaces are a beehive of activity swarming with thousands of strangers who drive from all points of the compass to work, then drive home again at night, leaving an empty concrete wasteland behind.

When you, your spouse, and/or your children converge on your home, if you are like most Americans you arrive frazzled by "the commute." You stagger into the house from the garage and turn on the television, going for days at a time without seeing the neighbors, and weeks between conversations with them. We seem to live life in a series of boxes. The house is a box, the office or factory is a box, and the box on wheels moves us between the two. Communication is mostly electronic: radio, television, telephone, computer, fax. It might just be possible to spend an entire day without conducting a face-to-face conversation with another human being. It is certainly possible to achieve total physical isolation for several hours at a time in our modern concrete and electronic wilderness. As a result, people become less real to us. The new reality is the information delivered by our various electronic devices. We know more and care more about Boris Yeltsin than we do our neighbor's alcoholic teenager.

According to *American Demographics* magazine, the American woman spends less than ten minutes a day with her newspaper, and men fare no better. Information is gathered in 15-second "sound bites" chosen for their emotional impact, rather than their relevance. Michael Deaver, the man who created Ronald Reagan's "image," asks how it is that the same people who were moved to demonstrate and weep in the streets over China's Tiananmen Square massacre of June 1989 could absorb the decision by President Bush only weeks later to continue normal relations with China's government? Deaver answers his own question by pointing out that we choose to exist in a highly emotional reality focused into a very short time span. Reality is defined by what we see on the tube today. As Deaver said to me, "Nothing is real unless it's on television. Much of what happens takes place because of television, and television has become a substitute for friends and family." Think about Deaver's observations as you turn on the television after a hard day.

The impact of the automobile and the television combine with the bulging size of our institutions to disconnect us from reality. During the early '80s, I worked in an advertising and PR firm in Tucson and Phoenix, consulting to political and commercial clients. The two locally-owned financial institutions our firm served were purchased by large California companies and are now in the hands of the Federal government. The four newspapers we represented are presently controlled by large corporations based in the Midwest or on the East Coast. All but one of the various real estate developments we worked with are now operated by the Resolution Trust Corporation (RTC). The convenience store chain we represented is currently managed by a Bankruptcy Court judge. The local bank that loaned money to our business has been acquired by a financial institution in Great Britain. And so it goes. Increasingly, we find ourselves at the mercy of decisions made in remote locations by individuals unknown to us who act without our knowledge or consent. Gary McDaniels, former president of a North Dakota bank, describes this as a web of influence and decision making which makes us feel helpless, struggling to survive. We cannot fully discover or understand the effects of this web, much less hold the web accountable for its actions; we can only follow the money.

In *The Work of Nations* by Robert Reich, the operation of a "global web" is graphically illustrated by how our money is divided up when we buy a typical American car. According to Reich, a Pontiac LeMans costs $20,000, from which General Motors sends $6,000 to South Korea for labor; $3,500 to Japan for components; $1,400 to Germany for engineering; $800 to Taiwan and Singapore for components; $500 to Britain for advertising; and $100 to Barbados and Ireland for data processing. We are isolated, cut off from our real community and living a false reality dictated by the decisions and opinions of people far removed from us.

Large institutions provide us with the necessities of life: the telephone company, the electric company, the oil company, the automobile company, the bank, the supermarket, the hospital, the airlines, and the media all enable us to survive. Each of these, however, operates under its own institutional wants and needs.

Actual decision makers in these institutions are often isolated from the customers they serve, depending on market research, financial reports, and the news media for the information they need to make decisions. The interests of the institution take precedence over the interests of the employees, the people who purchase the institution's products or serices, or even the well-being of the communities or countries in which the institution operates. There is often little concern for the common good and too much concern for what benefits the institution.

Government operates in ways similar to these other large organizations. Our children are educated, our interests defended, our transportation system operated, and the unfortunate among us cared for by massive governmental institutions, which relate to us no differently than the large commercial establishments. In fact, the typical government bureaucrat charged with the responsibility to deliver basic goods or services to the public is often even more insulated from the "customer" than his or her commercial counterpart. Consequently, government bureaucrats are often unresponsive to us.

Thanks to various provisions of the tax code, a peculiarly American phenomenon has evolved: the not-for-profit institution. These organizations are particularly prevalent in the arts, medical research, and educational fields. Not-for-profits operate much the same as any other large, impersonal organization, and because they depend for their existence on donations and (too often) government appropriations, they typically cooperate closely with commercial and governmental institutions.

Whatever their form or function, all of these institutions tend to become larger, more impersonal, and isolated from the world of those of us on the outside. Whether in the halls of Congress, City Hall, the corporate boardroom, or in relations between countries, the interests of these institutions are represented by flocks of lawyers, accountants, PR people, and lobbyists, and take precedence over the interests of the individual, the community, or the earth.

We live in cities and towns designed for the convenience of automobiles, not humans, and we work in environments dictated to us by impersonal organizations. We are isolated from each other, choosing to rely on electronic surrogate friends for our information.

Bill Moyers described the significance of this empty lifestyle in a September 1, 1991, *Washington Post Magazine* interview. "The contrived image is the dominant one in politics today," he said. "We are now living in a wall-to-wall culture of contrived images designed for the purposes of manipulation. Our entire society is built on a foundation of fiction." Moyers claimed that, as a consequence, we have lost the ability to think about our future or that of our children. Leaders do not lead. He referred to the recent crime bill passed in the Senate, saying, "It is a fraud. It will compound the problems it is supposed to solve, but everybody feels better. The purpose of politics and the media age is to make people feel good, not to think critically about what we need to do to solve our problems."

Our arrogant belief in our own PR has proven to be an illusion. We have traded our sense of community for lives of isolation, alone in our cars, alone in our offices, alone in front of the television. Communication is a phantom; instead of communicating, we are engulfed by bits of information shredded and strewn like confetti. It is no wonder we are confused.

We cope by living in a fog, defining success as possessions rather than personal achievements. We relate to each other on the basis of the circumscribed roles we play at home, in school, or on the job. We are quick to judge others using superficial standards of style, fashion, possessions, and expediency. We strive to gain acceptance by looking right, driving the right car, living in the right neighborhood, eating right, drinking right, watching the right TV programs, and voting for the right candidate — if we vote at all.

We stop looking ahead. We stop saving. We stop making the world a better place for coming generations. We are short-sighted. Our infrastructure decays, and we start a long downward spiral toward catastrophe.

Such are the results of our focus on money and things, instead of community. This near-sightedness leads to economic pressures that are rooted in fear. Fear becomes the currency with which we buy power. Candidates and political parties further divide us using fear. Some of us fear other races or religious groups. Others fear large corporations, and still others fear higher taxes. We each try to protect what is ours from "them."

This underlying anxiety and insecurity causes us to compensate by accumulation, conspicuous consumption, and aggressive behavior. We tend to assign responsibility for the problems which confront us to scapegoats. We waste time and energy in futile conflicts, lawsuits, strikes, and the

45

like. We fail to behave in a constructive manner; we fail to conserve our resources or build for the future.

Slowly, beginning in the 1960s, Americans began to realize that all was not right with the world. Young people began to question basic values. The Viet Nam experience called the invincibility of America into question. Drugs, the sexual revolution, and eventually the Watergate fiasco all contributed to the unease. The election of Jimmy Carter and his inept handling of the Iranians, coupled with "stagflation," tilted the scales. People, whether they admitted it or not, were worried. Fear became a fact of life.

The attitude, "ignore the problems and they will go away," triumphed in the election of Ronald Reagan. We sought to avoid the hard issues in an incredible spectacle of consumption during the '80s, fueled by tax cuts and increased defense spending, coupled with the theories of supply-side "Voodoo Economics." These reactions were really symptomatic of the underlying anxiety about what was, and is, happening in America and our denial of the reality of the situation. The fear factor hit full stride with the "Willie Horton" episode during the 1988 Presidential Campaign. (While out of jail on a Massachusetts prisoner furlough program, Horton raped a woman.) As a result, fear contributed substantially to the election of George Bush over Massachusetts Governor Michael Dukakis.

The problems, however, refuse to "just go away." Our country is not any better off now than it was in 1960, and in many ways it is worse. The United States as a country, and many (too many) of its citizens and the companies they work for, are living on borrowed time and borrowed money.

In this chapter I have tried to accomplish two things. The first is to describe that the failure to maintain a balanced economy based on "fair exchange value" prices is what went wrong in America in the last half of the twentieth century. Every other political and economic problem we face is basically a symptom of our flawed personal and national value system. The inability to recognize and correct the defects in our value system is the result of a changing cultural tide surging back and forth, drawn by arrogance and our loss of community.

Second, I hope to point out that even though fear may lead us to do foolish things in an effort to deny the existence of serious problems, even going so far as to help elect "feel good" politicians, fear will not provide an answer.

Chapter Four

The Worst Case

THE ISSUE THAT MATTERS IN AMERICA today is money. Our lifestyle is directly and negatively affected by foolish governmental policies and practices. We do not have to wait ten or fifteen years for the worst case to be realized — it is happening NOW!

The issue that matters probably will not be addressed in the upcoming 1992 presidential campaign or the one after in 1996. It will not be discussed because even though we all know deep in our guts just exactly how bad things are, no one running for office has the courage to honestly confront our problems.

They lack courage for several reasons:

1. The hurley-burley of politics is such that there really is not much time allotted for thoughtful contemplation or reflection, much less for problem solving.

2. The context within which politicians consider problems is such that those politicians are immersed in the detail of the current situation and seldom have the luxury to step back and look at the big picture; they cannot see the forest for the trees.

3. Politics is an adversarial game and the politician who goes too far out on a limb to address a situation or a problem is likely to find that limb sawed off.

4. Politicians communicate with constituents through

the media in the "15-second sound bite" — there is no real dialogue, so necessary for the development of real understanding.

5. Constituents communicate with politicians, if at all, on the most basic of levels — the irate letter, a contribution, or a vote for or against the politician.

6. Politicians have a generally low opinion of the voters' capability to understand the problems or any solution that might be offered.

7. Politicians may not be mental giants, themselves, being more interested in winning and holding office than in actual governance.

There is really no incentive to rock the boat. Beyond the seven reasons listed above, politicians generally lack political courage for the most important factor of all: Money!

Politics is expensive. Political candidates require lots of money to wage campaigns. Money comes most often from political action committees (PACs) funded by people with a vested interest in whatever it is that the politician might do to the status quo. This means that the people upon whom the candidate must depend for money are the very ones with the most to lose if the candidate addresses the real issues confronting this country. To appreciate how important money is, think about the U.S. Senator seeking reelection from a small state who will probably need 3 million dollars for the campaign. This means that for each of the 2,190 days of that Senator's term, he or she must obtain $1,369.86 from someone. Whoever puts up the money is bound to expect something in return. Do not hold your breath waiting for politicians to get up the courage to address the problems discussed in this book.

It gets worse. Most of the actual power in the system has been delegated to the employees of the government, affectionately known as bureaucrats. These people are not going to rock the boat either. They do not want to offend any prospective employers who might hire them once they complete their government service.

The only solution is to build a political consensus of agreement among the American people. Once a politician understands that his or her constituents agree on what direction the country should go, he or she will scramble to lead them in that direction. Once such a consensus is reached all the money from all the PACs cannot stop the momentum.

Creation of a political consensus is not easy. Even getting people to focus on the nature of the problem (money) is not easy. Money issues are left in the hands of economists, those people with advanced degrees from prestigious schools who are busy trying to write new economic analyses, win Nobel prizes, and appear regularly on public affairs shows. Economists tend to forget the basic reality in which the rest of us try to survive.

I believe that the objective of economics is off target. The objective should not be to control the economy; trying to control it is like trying to control the wind or the tide. Rather, the objective should be to discover how to assure that our economy is balanced. Adam Smith and George Peek, with their concepts of supply and demand and "fair exchange value," are closer to the truth of how economies work than any of the others.

Unless we put the economy back into balance by addressing the most basic issues of money, its value, the role of the individual, and the role of government, we are bound to be ravaged by economic depression, or subjected to social unrest, political terror, and personal disaster. The worst possible case bottom line will be the end of humankind's last best hope: the United States of America as we know it.

The 500 billion dollar swing in the net financial position of the United States over the eight years of the Reagan administration cost the United States economy 25,000 jobs for each one billion dollar shift, according to a Massachusetts Institute of Technology estimate. That adds up to 12,500,000 good jobs. There was a great deal of job creation during that same period — eight million or so new jobs, if you believe the administration — but most were "McJobs," not as good or high- paying as the ones that were lost. Even counting these new jobs, the arrival of the recession sent unemployment rates flying to seven percent as of July 1991, a three percent increase.

Charles Walters, writing in Acres U.S.A., a farm magazine devoted to eco-agriculture (farming that is both economically and ecologically sound) says, "A Johns Hopkins professor has computed that a one percent increase in unemployment rates increases [deaths] 36,887 annually . . . [causes] 4227 first admissions to mental hospitals and 3340 commitments to prison." If a depression occurs, we can expect unemployment rates in the 15 to 20 percent range.

Eventually, the misery index will become unbearable to the people of the United States of America. When that happens the situation could become truly explosive. Those who do not learn from the past are doomed to repeat it. Similar situations in other countries during this century have been resolved by scapegoating, armed revolution, genocide, and two world wars. Stalin, Hitler, Mussolini, and Mao took advantage of social, political, and economic collapse. In the United States during the last depression, a man named Huey Long capitalized on this type of unrest. He created a national following based on inflaming class consciousness and might have made it to the White House but for an assassin. President Franklin D. Roosevelt during the last depression presided over a significant expansion of federal government powers and intrusiveness, the effects of which haunt us even today. A national police force was established, known as the FBI; a national social welfare agency, our Social Security system, emerged on the premise that government is better able to make decisions regarding citizens' retirement and health care; and an intelligence community that was not supposed to spy within U.S. boundaries, but does anyway, developed into the CIA.

Already, we have witnessed the election of a president (George Bush) who was allowed by Michael Dukakis to use fear and race to clinch his victory. A former member of the Ku Klux Klan, David Duke, was unsuccessful in earlier attempts to win gubernatorial and U.S. Senate races in Louisiana, and is now a candidate for President, relying upon fear and racial hatred to propel his campaign. As we prepare for the 1992 election, the hot issue appears to be quotas, another code word for race. This is pointless. This is not the issue. Nor is the issue abortion, drugs, or Iraq. The real issue in 1992 is money and the value of our money. What will make a difference is whether my family and yours can make a decent living, own a home, pay for the kids' education, and leave behind a world a little better than what was left to us.

The signs are not good if you look around you. How bad can things get? Let's look at "the worst case" in one of our major industries — automobiles. One in seven American manufacturing jobs is related to the auto industry, and autos account for 4.1 percent of our gross national product, according to Kevin L. Kearns in a recent Washington Post article. He pointed out how bad the situation has become in this industry, stating that Japanese automakers have tripled their market share in the U.S. since 1978, and control 30 percent of our market. They are now building "transplant" cars inside our borders to take advantage of the cheap dollar and "Right to Work" states. In response, American automakers invested 170 billion dollars during the 1980s in a successful effort to improve product quality and worker productivity, drastically reducing the per-auto defect rate. Nevertheless, they continue to lose ground as American consumers become more loyal to Japanese brands.

The automobile industry directly employs 750,000 Americans and accounts for almost one-twentieth of the GNP. As Kearns said, "Transferring many of those jobs and much of that wealth-creating activity to foreign companies will have a devastating impact on America's economic future." Autos consume vast amounts of steel, plastics, textiles, rubber, and glass, and Kearns pointed out that without Detroit, the future of these secondary component manufacturers will also be at risk.

There are many reasons why transplants built in the United States cannot take up the slack in our auto industry. Among them: transplant factories are built by Japanese firms and financed by Japanese banks; tools, robots, and half of their parts suppliers come from Japan; profits go back to Japan; and U.S. taxes paid by these Japanese auto companies are much less than taxes paid by equivalent U.S. firms.

To make matters worse, the Japanese are deliberately overbuilding and targeting their excess capacity to the American market. In this way, said Kearns, "Japanese manufacturers can initiate fierce price competition — with the result that the big three will cede additional market share." Between 1984 and 1989, Detroit's capacity declined by about

1.2 million units and is predicted to decline another 700,000 units before the end of 1991.

To put this into perspective, consider that Japan limits foreign imports into the Japanese market to only five percent of the total number of autos sold in that country. They play on our court, but we are not allowed to play on theirs.

Unfortunately, the auto industry is just one of Japan's targets. Fred Barnes in a Readers Digest article identified a pattern of Japanese adversarial trade practices. For example, American construction firms are essentially excluded from Japan's construction market, although Japanese builders signed contracts worth 2.6 billion dollars of work in this country in 1988 alone. For another example, in 1980 Japan agreed to purchase 300 million dollars a year of U.S. auto parts, starting in 1981. They took eight years to reach that level. In a third case, the New York Stock Exchange automatically accepted four Japanese firms as primary dealers, whereas gaining admittance for three American securities firms to the Tokyo Stock Exchange required an act of Congress to overcome Japanese resistance. These are just three of many Japanese antagonistic trade practices and just one "worst case" scenario.

When will we decide we have reached the limit? When will we decide how much debt is too much? How many people can be out of work before the economy collapses? How many working people with a lack of funds can be cut off from medical care, or bankrupted by it, before the system is judged a failure? How many people can we afford to keep in jail? How many non-producing government employees will the taxpayers put up with?

How many rules and regulations can our bureaucrats promulgate before the economy chokes? How much garbage can we dump before we run out of landfill space? How much gunk can we pump into the air before it is too dirty to breathe and the combination of acid rain, ozone depletion, and the like make life unlivable? How many more gallons of raw sewage and chemical waste, or tons of nitrogen and potassium, can be dumped into the water before there is no water to drink and the oceans die? How much money can we print before hyperinflation sets in?

When will the "misery index" become too much to bear and then what will happen?

As things go from bad to worse, the effect is cumulative and the impact on individuals accelerates. Each of us was taught about the effect of compounding interest rates in high school. This rule applies equally well to the reverse situation.

Beginning in 1948, when the earlier 1942 War Stabilization Act expired, the U.S. economy began a slow, steady abandonment of Peek's principle of "fair exchange value." A Farm Act was passed in 1948 that contained provisions designed to assure that "fair exchange value" operated in the agricultural sector of the economy; after one year, it discounted the "fair exchange value" equations and provided for indexing of these equations by recomputing them every ten years. Thus, the original 1948 discounts have been compounded every decade.

The effects are plain for all to see. There is not enough earned income in the American economy and borrowed funds are replacing the shortfall in earned income. What money is available is often misused: the situation has been made worse by a series of idiotic actions such as the deregulation of the S&L industry; lowering the value of the dollar relative to other currencies; and development of the junk bond as a source of very high interest money (really just very expensive loans) for dealmakers. Equally foolish has been the explosion of government, business, and consumer borrowing; periods of high inflation; chronic failure to balance the federal budget; the trade deficit; and free trade practices that practically encourage "dumping" (the practice of selling goods like minivans and computer screens at less than it costs to produce them, in order to expand market share and drive American companies out of business) by foreign manufacturers.

The combination of all the above creates a disaster which is about to befall the American people. A recession has been underway for over a year, but the politicians will probably find a short term way to end that recession before the '92 election. The problems will continue to fester however, despite their efforts.

The Savings and Loan crisis demonstrated exactly how fragile our institutions are, and how expensive it can be to correct our mistakes. If you liked the Savings and Loan crisis, you will love the bank crisis coming up next. There will be a major depression before the end of this century, if nothing is done to correct the current situation.

The remainder of this book will examine the political process and offer a set of policy solutions for America's worsening problems. Most important, it will also outline a game plan for anyone concerned enough about the future of this country to step in and reclaim the power of the people ordained to us by our Constitution.

PART TWO

GOVERNMENT
& POLITICS

I repeat . . . that all power is a trust — that we are accountable for its exercise — that from the people, and for the people, all springs, and all must exist.

Benjamin Disraeli

Vivian Grey bk. vi, ch. 7

Chapter Five

Why Bother?

LIKE ALMOST EVERYTHING ELSE in our lives, we take government for granted. It appears to be a given—unchangeable and permanent. Yet news stories lay witness to how fragile institutions and governments really are. Beginning with Lech Walesa in Poland and Corazon Aquino in the Philippines, and culminating most recently with Boris Yeltsin in Russia, a wind of change has swept through the world. All bets are off. Everything is up for grabs. You probably think it could not happen here, but think again.

What if the Federal Deposit Insurance Corporation failed and millions of Americans were unable to withdraw money from their bank accounts? Or perhaps, if the FDIC were to be bailed out in similar fashion to the Federal Savings and Loan Insurance Corporation, what would happen if the country faced another depression or a siege of hyperinflation? If the worst case becomes a reality in the United States, we could easily witness a major change in our form of government. Unfortunately, such a change might make things worse.

Even if we escape the current trend of convulsive change, we are not immune to the process of evolution and change that occurs every day, month to month, year to year. As H.L. Mencken said, "The public demands certainties, but there are no certainties." Government and society today would not be recognizable to our country's founders. Change is unrelenting—some things get better, some get worse. The appearance of stability and permanence is an illusion.

In Thomas Jefferson's day, slavery appeared to be a permanent institution. Teddy Roosevelt never dreamed of anything like Social Security. Harry Truman never rode a jet airplane while in office, much less "Air Force One." Lyndon Johnson would not have considered visiting China. The Berlin Wall was a permanent fixture to Gerald Ford, and Ronald Reagan thought the Soviet Union was "the evil empire." Things change.

One hundred years ago there were no freeways, televisions, or nuclear weapons. Fifty years ago there were no weather satellites, A.I.D.S. patients, or astronauts. Ten years ago there were no drug wars, free elections in Eastern Europe, or anti-smoking ordinances.

At the turn of the century we had no Federal Reserve Board, income tax, or the IRS. At the end of World War I, there was no FBI, and World War II was fought without a CIA. NASA was nonexistent in 1950, as was the Department of Energy. We saw no Medicare or Medicaid in 1960, and no one had heard of a Drug Czar in 1970.

Stop for a moment and think about the difference all of these changes have made in your life. Which have made life better? Which worse? Are these agencies necessary? What if they suddenly went away?

Everything discussed so far in this chapter has been influenced or created through government policy. Some of the issues, slavery for example, divided the country, while others made less of an impact. Whatever the issue, our society is in constant change, arbitrated in large part by our governmental institutions.

People who do not care about the kinds of issues outlined above can afford to disconnect themselves from political decision making. If one or more of these issues affects you or me and our families, however, we should pay attention to the political process. In the final analysis, every aspect of life ranging from work to relationships, money to health, is subject to government influence and/or manipulation.

The quality of our children's education, the safety of our neighborhood streets, and the security of our savings accounts are all political questions. So are issues like the quality of the air we breathe, the price of the gas running our cars, and our access to the information in this book. Politics intrudes into all areas of life.

For better or for worse, this intrusion is presumed to take place with our consent. A long line of political thinkers, beginning in the 17th century with Hutcheson, Locke, and Hume, endorsed the concept of the social contract as the legitimate foundation upon which to build a government.

Locke's "Second Treatise of Government" and "Essay Concerning Human Understanding" were influential documents in 18th century America. They define a natural law referred to by Thomas Jefferson when he said, "We hold these truths to be self-evident, that all men are created equal, that they are endowed by their Creator with certain unalienable Rights, that among these are Life, Liberty and the pursuit of Happiness."

The social contract is identified as the basis of government in the Declaration of Independence, immediately following the definition of natural law. Jefferson said, ". . . that to secure these rights, governments are instituted among men, deriving their just powers from the consent of the governed." The social contract is interpreted to preserve natural freedom, the unalienable rights identified in the Declaration, within the context of a government.

61

The social contract as theorized by Locke is not a contract between the rulers or leaders and the people. Instead, the contract is by and between the people, who then delegate certain of their powers to the rulers. The rulers in turn exercise those delegated powers on behalf of the people, as Trustees acting in a fiduciary capacity. The delegation of powers by the people to the rulers is only valid so long as the rulers are faithful to the people; they must exercise their delegated powers for the benefit of the people in accordance with the underlying principles of natural law.

Locke believed that each person ratified the ongoing social contract by giving "tacit consent" to his or her government. He recognized that society is too complex to tolerate a renegotiation of the social contract by each passing generation. Interestingly, Jefferson advocated that governments ought not to be allowed to obligate future generations on the theory that such debt or obligation was a violation of the implicit assumptions of natural law. Had Jefferson prevailed, the incredible deficits being incurred by the U.S. government would have been precluded.

Although Locke believed that unanimous consent of the population is required to establish a social contract, day-to-day decision making can and should be undertaken on the basis of majority rule. Locke did not clearly define how to protect the rights of minorities in his writings; however, he defined certain limits on the activities of government. Among these limits he listed equal application of law to all members of society, taxation only with the consent of the governed, and vesting supreme power in the legislature, which cannot delegate its prerogatives. Modern government, which has levied indirect, hidden taxes and delegated rule-making and regulation-writing to unelected bureaucrats, seems to stretch the limits Locke would impose.

Finally, Locke believed in the right of the people to revolt when government became too aggressive. Jefferson invoked this right in the Declaration of Independence, which is presented in entirety in Appendix D:

"That whenever any Form of Government becomes destructive of these ends, it is the Right of the People to alter or abolish it, and to institute new Government, laying its foundations on such principles and organizing its powers in such form, as to them shall seem most likely to effect their Safety and Happiness. Prudence, indeed, will dictate that Governments long established should not be changed for light and transient causes; and accordingly all experience hath shewn, that mankind are more disposed to suffer, while evils are sufferable, than to right themselves by abolishing the forms to which they are accustomed. But when a long train of abuses and usurpations, pursuing invariably the same Object evinces a design to reduce them under absolute Despotism, it is their right, it is their duty, to throw off such Government, and to provide new Guards for their future security."

The events of the past few years in Poland, the Philippines, and the former U.S.S.R. are a modern ratification of the natural law and social contract approach which provides the philosophical foundation for the United States of America. This philosophy is alive and well not only in Warsaw, Moscow, and Manila, but also in New York, Des Moines, and Minneapolis.

Why bother about government? Bother, because government depends for its existence upon your consent and mine. If we want good government and a just, stable society, we must take an interest in creating and maintaining those institutions.

Chapter Six

Politics: A Complex of Social Relations

WEBSTER'S SEVENTH NEW COLLEGIATE Dictionary defines "politics" (if you skip the first several lines referring to the art or science of government, competition for power, etc., and go on to the final definition) as "the total complex of relations between people in society." It is this final and broadest definition which is used in this book. Politics includes everything from choosing a President to who sits in the office with a view at your workplace. Relations with the neighbors, relations between nations, and the price of bread are all political questions. Building inspectors, police officers, teachers, tax collectors, garbage collectors, office managers, shift supervisors, and news reporters are all politicians, and so are you and I, because everyone alive is engaged to some degree in this complex of relations in society.

Many people are turned off by politics. They refuse to register or vote, and disdain the political process. These people ignore the news, dismiss the candidates, and often resent the government. Whether they know it or not, their acts are political: not to decide is to decide.

It is impossible to escape the daily reality of political interdependence. Those political dropouts who try to ignore formal politics still have to pay taxes, are still regulated by laws, and still work and play within the societal infrastructure. All they have done is give others the right to make their decisions, thus control their lives.

There is another type of political dropout, and that is the person who feels overwhelmed by the hopelessness of making any difference. They see other people wearing fancy clothes and driving expensive cars, running cities and making decisions, and they feel powerless. They say, "I don't have a college degree, I can't afford a lawyer, I don't understand economics, and I don't have time to learn the system because I have to make a living." But by dropping out of the political process, these folks, too, have turned over their powers to others—they have ignored their right to control their quality of life.

From President to unemployed hitchhiker, wherever you stand on the political continuum, the following statements are true:

Politics, the total complex of relations between people in society, has a massive impact on the quality of our life.

Dropping out as a consequence of alienation, intimidation, ignorance, or laziness merely gives others the right to make decisions which control the quality of our life.

Chapter Seven

Power is the Reality

THE REALITY OF GOVERNMENT and politics is power. Government has the power, using military force if necessary, to control the flow of money and information in our society. Government has the power to determine what conduct, speech, publications, entertainment, occupations, and products are or are not acceptable, so long as it does not exceed the limits of our social contract, as defined in the Declaration of Independence and federal and state constitutions. (The limits of that social contract can be, and often are, stretched from time to time by amendment and interpretation, however.)

Power is difficult to pin down, and its trappings are often mistaken for it. John F. Kennedy possessed all the symbols of power, but whomever designed his assassination had more actual power. During the era of Prohibition, the Justice Department, FBI, and local law enforcement agencies had the law on their sides, but the thirst of Americans for alcohol proved more powerful and eventually changed the law. Those who uphold the laws of our country all have power, but so do those willing to break the law or ignore it. American women obtained abortions before *Roe v. Wade*, and they will obtain them again if it is overturned. Any American who wants to can buy cocaine, regardless of the laws against it and the heroic efforts made to enforce those laws. Do not forget, Americans refused to drive 55 miles per hour.

As a people we agree that we need a government and we believe in the form of government defined by the Constitution. Our representatives—both elected and appointed—operate that government as Trustees for us. Its operation, however, is complicated by the way power must be shared. With the Constitution, we the people have delegated a little power to many different institutions within the government. No one has absolute power.

For over 200 years the various players in our government have fought for their share of delegated power. The formal division of power is in a constant state of flux, depending on the relative strength of the competing personalities and the current interpretation of the Constitution. Beyond the power delegated to government and administered through the machinery of the Constitution, however, there are other kinds of power at work in the system.

First, the power of money. Money is the mother's milk of government and politics—people need it, want it, and will do almost anything to get it. With enough money a person (or a country, or a company) can hire someone to do almost anything. Money can buy us special access to the Trustees operating the machinery of government who act in our behalf, and sometimes buys us favorable decisions. We have all witnessed the resignation of a Vice President caught taking money (Spiro Agnew) and seen video tapes of Senators taking money; most of us believe these represent only the tip of the iceberg. Money talks.

Fred Barnes, in an August 1990 *Reader's Digest* article, reported that the Japanese spent 43 million dollars on lobbying in 1989. Taking their American subsidiaries into consideration, they spent an additional 60 million dollars for lawyers, publicists, and advisors. According to Barnes, "Over the years these have included some of the best-connected people in Washington: former Democratic National Chairman Charles Manatt, former U.S. trade representative William Eberle, former Oklahoma Congressman James R. Jones, and former CIA director William Colby." Again, money talks.

Second, the power of information. What we don't know can, and often does, hurt us. What we do know changes how we act. The same can be said for elected or appointed officials who act as Trustees of our power. The recent Charles Keating fiasco is a good example of information power.

The five Senators investigated by the Senate Ethics Committee, known as the "Keating Five," had requested a meeting with Savings and Loan regulators to ask them for a report on Lincoln Savings & Loan which was supposed to have been released almost four months earlier. Feeling threatened, these regulators released a transcript of the meeting instead, framing it in such a way as to accuse the Senators of acting improperly, as if a fat-cat campaign contributor such as Charles Keating were receiving special treatment from them. (In fact, the Senators were probably doing their jobs, representing the interests of the thousands employed by Keating's businesses, as well as returning a favor to a contributor.) This was an intentional effort to hide the fact that they, as regulators, were failing to resolve the Savings and Loan situation. These regulators were not concerned with Keating or the Senators, they were creating a diversion, hoping to hide the fact that their incompetent management of the Savings and Loan industry would force the American public to bail out the system at a cost approaching 200 billion dollars. Their judicious release of superfluous information, coupled with the current political witch-hunting mood, succeeded in diverting the country from recognizing the real crime.

Third, the power of the press, which includes print as well as electronic media. Anyone doubting the power of the press should examine the careers of Richard Nixon and Gary Hart.

In the best sense, the press can be compared to a spotlight that exposes the truth of a situation. In the worst sense, the press is used and abused by people with axes to grind who are assassins of character, not just tellers of lies. Remember that the press is a business dependent upon attracting readers or an audience to survive. It is intensely competitive, characterized by a short attention span, and staffed by reporters who are usually well-intentioned, but whose egos often direct their coverage of a story. The press is a power which is ignored at great peril.

Fourth, the power of tradition and custom. We are all programmed throughout life to be members of this society. For complex reasons I do not fully understand, I was one of thousands who stood, cheering and crying, at the victory parade of soldiers returned from the Persian Gulf. I stand and sing when the national anthem is played, I vote in every election, and I like football more than a rational human being should. None of us can fully comprehend the degree to which custom and tradition guide our actions and those of our neighbors.

Fifth, the power of expectation. Whether we live in the White House or a shelter for the homeless, we all live in a web of expectation. These expectations cause us to act in certain ways and to anticipate others' actions, which can have positive or negative consequences. For example, if you correctly expect another driver to stop at a red light, you may proceed unimpeded through your own green light. If, however, your expectation is wrong, it may cause you to err (by not paying attention as you approach the intersection), with horrible consequences. The Keating Five never expected regulators to release meeting notes or to level accusations of impropriety. Their expectations led them to the assumption that they were doing their jobs, but resulted in an ethics investigation.

Sixth, the uniquely American power of the interest group. Millions of Americans join interest groups ranging from the Sierra Club and the American Civil Liberties Union to the Heritage Foundation and the National Rifle Association. These groups wield incredible power to make government act in certain ways, or to change the way the rest of us think and behave. Interest groups are established around almost any issue, and for many, the focus goes beyond public policy to include education, research, or charity. Some groups act as trade associations for economic interests, or labor unions seeking to advance the cause of working people. Whether they work together, independently, or oppose one another, interest groups can be a power to reckon with.

Seventh, the power of religion. Many of the original colonial governments were established and nurtured for religious purposes. Religion has been, is, and will continue to be a power nexus in American society. The First Amendment to the Constitution provides for separation of church and state, but our money says, "In God We Trust." The abortion dispute is frequently cast in a religious context, and some groups believe that the current social contract should be changed to assure that the United States operates as a "Christian Nation." Because organized religion has a strong asset base, millions of members, and the will to pursue its point of view in the public policy arena, it will remain as a powerful force in America.

Finally, there is the power of political parties. The

parties have been in decline for some time, attributed to several factors. The most important negative influences on them are the rise of television and the demise of political patronage as a means of rewarding loyal workers. Television makes it possible to receive political information in real time, giving viewers the illusion that the information they receive is complete and accurate. The local political activist who used to depend on the party for political information now turns to C-SPAN or CNN, lessening the value of party membership and party loyalty. The former worker who spent hundreds of hours on behalf of the party can no longer look forward to employment after the campaign, so he or she spends time and energy elsewhere.

Other reasons for the parties' slump include the birth of single issue interest groups and the creation of the political action committee. Both provide an alternative way to funnel money and support to the candidates, outside of regular party channels.

Political parties remain important, nevertheless. Even though the typical party platform is so broad it can either appeal to or offend virtually anyone, the party remains the only reliable way to secure ballot access and implied credibility for candidates.

Due to state laws, minor or third party efforts to qualify for ballot positions are severely handicapped, and if a party cannot get its candidate on the ballot, it is doomed. Therefore, their monopoly on ballot access continues to provide the Democrats and the Republicans a reason to exist. In Presidential campaigns these two parties have also managed to get on the gravy train for federal funds collected as an income tax check-off, which creates another reason for their continued existence. Thus, although it is limited, the Democratic and Republican Parties still exercise legitimate power.

The formal delegation of power to the government through the Constitution, taken together with these eight external forces, acts in a political equilibrium. At any point in time on any issue, forces are brought to bear to achieve an objective, while other forces are mobilized to prevent that objective from being achieved.

In the middle of these contending forces are the elected and appointed officials to whom we have made a delegation of power and who act as our fiduciary representatives. These officials have their own agenda, which is to be powerful. For an official, power is defined as holding political office, whether elected or appointed. At their best, these "public servants" try to act based on what they believe to be right. They seek to understand the philosophy behind our system of government, and they work hard to discharge their fiduciary responsibilities. At their worst, they are unable to hold any but a political job, they are motivated by greed or lust for the trappings of power, and they abuse the rights of the people they are supposed to serve.

This is the reality of government and politics in America today. The soup of delegated power, competing interests in and out of government, challenging issues, and personal fortunes of our various officials is constantly bubbling. It is impossible to dominate this system. No one group has the ability to exercise absolute power. No one interest can be assured of victory. No one factor is so important that it can overcome all of the other factors.

Although domination of the process is effectively prevented, some observers feel the dynamic of the system creates inevitable paralysis. The next chapter explains why they are wrong.

Chapter Eight

Prospects for America

BEING RIGHT IS NO GUARANTEE that your point of view will prevail. Others are equally sure that you are mistaken.

Being in the majority is no guarantee that your point of view will prevail. Our system of checks and balances based on the division of power could allow a small minority to defeat you.

Having money is no guarantee that your point of view will prevail. There is always money for the other side, and our information systems tend to present at least two, if not more, sides of an issue to the electorate.

Having the media on your side does not always work, either. Many Americans are rightly suspicious of them. To make matters worse, the media seldom agree on anything, anyway. Even if a portion of the media are on your side, some will work against you.

Getting a law passed cannot even assure success. The law will inevitably be challenged because it violates some part of our social contract—the U.S. Constitution—and the judges might agree. If it is upheld in the courts, it still may be destroyed by the bureaucracy. Congress regularly passes laws which are signed by the President, upheld by the courts, and forgotten by everyone else. One example is a program mandated by Congress to force the USDA to support family farmers during the farm crisis of the early 1980s. The USDA decided to ignore the law and focus instead on foreclosures to remedy the crisis. Four years had passed before farmers could obtain judicial relief to force compliance. In the meantime, thousands of families saw their life's work sold at auction, and hundreds were driven to suicide by the very people instructed to help them.

Another example was reported in a front page story of the September 22, 1991, *Washington Post*. The House and Senate, after much debate and consideration, passed a bill to protect the environment, which the President signed. During the debate, the President had repeatedly offered a series of measures for inclusion in the bill, which Congress specifically and intentionally rejected. Now, several months later, the Environmental Protection Agency is writing regulations, which carry the force of law, containing many of the President's specific recommendations that Congress had considered and rejected. Using the processes of the Administrative Procedures Act, the bureaucrats in the EPA are contradicting the will of Congress by changing the way utilities can account for pollution control equipment, in ways which make it possible for many utilities to avoid installing the equipment at all. In effect, bureaucratic changes can thwart the legislative intent of Congressionally approved bills. This kind of underhanded activity goes on daily in virtually every department of the federal government.

Even if you succeed in getting a law passed and signed, upheld in court, and enforced by the bureaucrats, it might still be sidetracked by other statutes and agencies. Remember the Snail Darter? It was an obscure, tiny fish whose threatened existence stopped a major Tennessee Valley Authority dam project, and helped establish the Endangered Species Act, to boot.

People who live and work inside Washington D.C.'s

"beltway" and run the federal government are becoming as cynical and alienated by all of this as the rest of us who fund the government with our tax dollars. The system seems incapable of doing what must be done to assure its survival. There appears to be a crisis of vision and will. Perhaps it is a crisis of design and structure in the system, which is a more attractive alternative for people who have limited vision and lack political will.

The next two sections of this book define a process and point of view which, together with the series of issue, funding, and policy initiatives presented, can provide the vision and mobilize the will to make the existing structure of government work the way it can and should. What is required is a way of seeing, understanding, and then addressing the various problems confronting America, rather than the current approach of slapping a band-aid on whatever appears most pressing at the moment. This comprehensive program must first address the most fundamental issues facing us and threatening our national security: the value of money, the operation of our economy, trade, taxation, and the operation of government in a manner consistent with the existing social contract.

Government as it now operates exceeds the implicit terms of our social contract. It is involved in a variety of issues and endeavors which are expensive, counterproductive, and wasteful. The policy and economic solutions offered here will probably not be acceptable to everyone. For those who disagree with these solutions, the final chapters define a process of political education and participation which can make it possible for any group to attempt to achieve a broad consensus based on its vision.

In the final analysis, the governmental structure currently in place is workable, with some minor adjustments. It will require you, me, and other concerned citizens to make government more responsible and accountable to its people. We have suffered long enough as unwitting victims paying the price for our leaders' mistakes and our own inattention.

PART THREE

HOLISTIC POLITICS

There must be no tempering with justice, with the rule of the weight of the measure you employ; an even scale, a true balance, a full bushel, a full pint-measure . . .

Leviticus 19:35-36

Chapter Nine

Where Do We Go From Here?

NOW FOR THE GOOD NEWS. We can make a difference. It is not too late to start. Building a political consensus is possible, and we can Reinvent America in time to stave off disaster.

America's citizens are capable of understanding the economy, money, and the value of money. We can create a balanced economy based upon the tried-and-true principles espoused by Adam Smith and George Peek. An economy utilizing "fair exchange value" will operate in harmony with natural law. Although it is not possible to control all aspects of an economy, and it is foolish to try, it is possible to live, earn, reproduce, and have fun without destroying the environment or our neighbors. We can do all of this without creating a police state or a central planning bureau to make our choices for us.

People leading productive lives in a balanced economy will achieve their full potential and will usually choose to forego substance abuse, violent crime, or threats to each other's safety. We do not require a government that regulates every aspect of our lives. We can educate our children, feed all of our citizens, and provide adequate medical care without bankrupting ourselves, our employers, or our government. We can do all of this and more, if we choose.

Of course, the Constitution and the Bill of Rights give you the right to decide differently. We could as easily choose to do none of the things listed above. We can choose to continue on as before and experience the worst case scenario described in Chapter Four.

The third part of this book is a road map of the process that must be followed by a significant minority of Americans if we are to rescue our country. There is nothing magic about what is proposed here. It is just common sense. This common sense approach to solving the crises of the '90s will work if enough of us try it.

Succeeding does not require people to become full time political activists. It does mean, at a minimum, that you will think about the issues raised, the solutions offered, and the processes recommended in *Reinventing America*. Having thought about all of that, it presumes that you will become involved in society in some way beyond just reading this book. You might choose to join a club, work with young people, or become active in your church. You can also register to vote, go back to school, get a job. Or, you could go "whole hog" and become actively engaged in an issue, run for office, or help someone else to run.

The following pages suggest a different way of thinking about politics and issues. It could be dubbed "holistic politics."

All aspects of political and governmental life are interdependent with each other. It is not possible to make decisions to protect the environment, as an example, without recognizing the effect those decisions would have on all other aspects of our daily life. Consider that Congress and the Environmental Protection Agency have decided to change what is an acceptable standard of chemical emissions. The objective is a good one, to protect the air. What isn't realized is that thousands of dry cleaners all over America will be put out of business. Not only will small family-operated cleaners no longer be feasible, it is going to be more inconvenient and cost more money for you to get your clothes cleaned. Of course our environment needs to be protected. However, how much thought was given to those thousands of families, and how they are going to survive once their livelihood is taken away from them? This is a modest example of what happens when only the parts are considered, ignoring the whole.

Following the discussion of holistic politics, I will define exactly how I believe a government should be run. I start with the most basic issue, money and its value, and go from there. You may or may not agree with my ideas, but I hope that you will agree with at least some of what I have to say (especially about how we value our money) and begin to work with me and others to implement the changes I recommend. These chapters are really the guts of what I call "Reinventing America."

As you go through the rest of the book, take everything I say and consider that I may very well be wrong. It is not important that you agree with me, because I would rather have a thoughtful dialogue with someone who disagrees with me than receive his or her blind acceptance of my ideas. I look forward to hearing from you and I will attempt to answer everyone who writes. Hopefully you are learning as you read this and you, in turn, can teach me. You will find my address in the back of the book.

Chapter Ten

The Political Ecosystem

WE LIVE IN A SOCIETY OF PARTS. Typically, we only focus on one or two parts at a time. You have heard the old saying that it is hard to see the forest for the trees. That is a fairly accurate representation of our current situation. We concern ourselves with issues such as education, crime, government ethics, defense, agriculture, or the budget on a case-by-case basis. We rarely try to relate all of these issues into a cohesive whole. This is at the least an incomplete way of thinking about things, and at its worst dangerous.

The situation should be viewed as a whole, not as unrelated fragments. If the interests of the whole are not considered, the solution to a problem within any single segment can make the whole sicker.

My favorite example of this is agriculture. Harry Truman declared the end of World War II on December 31, 1946. Two years later, on December 31, 1948, the War Stabilization Act of 1942 expired. The Stabilization Act had provided for imposition of Peek's principle of "fair exchange value" to assure that the economy functioned in balance so that maximum economic strength could be brought to bear on the war effort.

During 1948, a Farm Act was passed to replace the Stabilization Act of 1942. This new Act applied a watered-down version of "fair exchange value" which does not work.

Truman and his friends did not intend to make a mess of American agriculture, they were only trying to establish a "cheap food" policy and open American markets to exporters of agricultural products so those countries could make sales, generate hard currency, and service their debt to U.S. banks. Everyone was supposed to win.

To accomplish this "noble" purpose, the Farm Act eventually forced American farmers to produce at less than their cost of production. As of February, 1991, USDA projected costs for American farmers to grow and harvest a bushel of wheat are $4.14, while the most that bushel of wheat will be sold for is projected to be about $3.00. Forty odd years after passage of the Farm Act, and the face of American agriculture has been execrably changed.

The family farm which Thomas Jefferson thought central to a viable democracy is almost extinct. Today there are fewer than 1,000,000 families living on farms. Those farmers who have survived have determined that the only way to make it is to practice the "economics of scale" and the "economics of welfare."

If making a living on the old family farm proves impossible, the economics of scale dictate that a farmer grow his or her way out of the problem. Buy more land, automate, apply chemicals to enhance production, and produce more at a lower unit cost. A tremendous establishment has been created to help farmers do this.

These "improvements" are paid for using the economics of welfare: subsidies and low interest loans financed or guaranteed by the government. Billions of dollars of government money are devoted to this misguided effort each year.

These survival strategies have had several unintended consequences. To artificially increase per acre yield, farmers have used more and more chemical fertilizers, pesticides, and plant foods. At one point, a farmer could not qualify for those "life saving" subsidies and low interest loans unless he or she used the "approved" farming techniques, i.e., used vast quantities of chemical additives. The result has been severe depletion of topsoil, ground water pollution, consumer fear, damage to wildlife, and accumulation of pesticides in the natural food chain.

Survival farming requires large quantities of fresh water. Irrigation dramatically increases yields but equally dramatically depletes fresh ground water stored over thousands of years. The ground actually subsides, destroying roads, houses, and property. Eventually, we will run out of water to pump.

Because of economic pressures and government subsidies, inappropriate crops are being grown in certain regions of the country. For example, too much cotton (a very water-intensive crop) is grown in the desert and too much tobacco is grown, period. Unfortunately, growing these cash crops is the only way many farmers can eke out a living.

A new class of non-farmers has evolved to take advantage of rules, regulations, and various payment programs which the government has designed to "manage" agriculture. Many of these people are the very ones the system is trying not to help. They are already wealthy enough to afford lawyers and accountants to mine the assistance programs, extract dollars using the loopholes and subsidies, and refine the profitability of not-farming to the highest degree.

A horde of well-meaning bureaucrats is depleting the agricultural vitality of the country. Among their many ill-conceived practices, they tend to micro-manage the poor farmer by forcing compliance with meaningless regulations, and supporting survival farming as described above. This agricultural system is failing.

There is not enough money or institutional wisdom to support this "Sovietization of American Agriculture." Money is chronically short. The USDA has proven that if you lose a little money at low volumes of production, you lose even more at higher volumes. They have created huge food surpluses, which are stored at taxpayer expense while hunger remains a world problem. For a better understanding of why this is happening, re-read Chapter Two, "The Value of Money."

For a time, the urge for larger and larger farms created a demand for land, driving up land prices. As land prices climbed, so did its collateral value to secure larger government loans, hiding a multitude of sins in the process. Eventually, the bubble burst and it was no longer possible to pay the interest on government loans, much less retire the principal. During the early '80s, the specter of the farm auction became familiar to all of America.

As pressure increased on the bureaucracy, it reacted predictably. The farmer was made the scapegoat for failed USDA policy, although farmers had just been following bureaucratic advice and regulations. Farmers were abused so mercilessly that a judge in North Dakota eventually had to issue a Permanent Injunction in 1983 to stop illegal government foreclosure proceedings aimed at 77,000 family farmers. To really appreciate this ruthlessness, rent the video movie "Country," starring Jessica Lange and Sam Shepard.

The rural society which supports the farmer has also been heavily stressed. Over fifty years, almost 80 percent of farmers have been driven off their land. The domino effect on small town businesses, professionals, banks, and so on, has been no less devastating. These people, or at least their children, have had to move to cities, further loading overburdened city infrastructure and leaving rural, small town America to slowly fade away.

As more and more food is imported into this country from abroad, an odd thing is happening. Today, there is more imported pork from Poland sold in the city of Chicago, described by poet Carl Sandburg as the "Hog butcher of the world," than one finds American pork. In fact, the Chicago stockyards have been closed. Meanwhile, the people in Poland, the former U.S.S.R, and other Eastern Bloc countries spend a good portion of their lives standing in line to buy food. More dramatic examples can be found: many backward countries have populations who suffer from malnutrition, yet those countries export food to the United States. Something is clearly out of balance.

Another example of unintended consequences can be found with the deregulation of the Savings and Loan industry. Intended to spur development, reduce government intervention, and stimulate the economy, deregulation instead will cost taxpayers at least 500 billion dollars, not to mention as yet uncalculated costs to private investors, depositors, and newly unemployed people.

Yet a third example is Social Security and the rest of the entitlement programs. Today about seven percent of the gross national product is sucked up by Social Security and other programs, yet most people under 40 fear they will be left holding the bag when it comes time for them to collect benefits. In an effort to hold down the burden of government on taxpayers (and to avoid a tax revolt), remaining government tax collections have declined from 20 percent to about 12 percent of the GNP since Social Security was created. Spending, however, has not declined. Thus, our federal government spends at a rate of about 23 to 25 percent of the GNP but only collects about 19 percent. This is one reason for the federal deficit.

At the same time, people cannot afford to live on Social Security alone, so government added Medicare and then Medicaid, the mother of all boondoggles. Administrators noticed that their system was unable to cover the expenses incurred, and they imposed a maximum rate of pay on the hospitals. They decided to pick on hospitals rather than doctors, because the doctors' powerful and well-funded union, the American Medical Association (AMA), is difficult to fight. The system of payment government administrators devised is based on a series of over 400 illnesses classified as "Diagnostic Related Groupings," and specifies the maximum allowable charge for accepted treatment procedures. The difference between what the government will pay and what is actually spent by hospitals to provide these treatments is collected from you and me (or our employers and insurance companies). This has caused the cost of insurance to shoot up to a point where many of us can no longer afford to buy it.

Put another way, hospitals are dependent upon doctors for survival, there are a limited number of doctors, and it is doctors who refer patients to hospitals. To compete for patients, hospitals install specialized, high-ticket equipment and perform specialized, high-ticket procedures; one city, for example, may have three or four open-heart surgery teams, when only one or two are called for. The costs of this overlapping are passed on to patients with insurance, which are of course passed on to all insurance consumers as expensive premiums. This process is known in the industry as "cost shifting." It is another example of what happens when the law of supply and demand explained so well by

Adam Smith is abused by artificial restriction on supply, in this case restricted by the AMA.

Now, more than 37 million of us are uninsured. Hospitals, nursing homes, and insurance companies are cutting corners, fleecing patients and each other, and going out of business at a record pace. Doctors have become politicized, as has the provision of medical care, with a decline in quality as the consequence. The United States now spends more per capita than any other country on medical care, and the system is in danger of collapse.

Those examples should be enough to show you that we function in a system where the solution to any one problem can debilitate the whole system if the interests of the whole are not considered and taken into account. In other words, this political system functions as an ecosystem, where each component is connected to all others, a change in one manifesting as a change in all.

Each term Congress, the President, and various federal agencies do the best they can to deal with the issues confronting them. Being human, they deal with the most pressing issues first: election, re-election, and job security. Other "important" issues like Senate and House office assignments and committee appointments too often come next in the hierarchy. When it finally comes time to deal with the real issues confronting the nation, our elected and appointed officials attack them one at a time, and in the context of election, reelection, and job security. As a result, each issue is dealt with independently of the overall situation facing the country, and without consideration of how one decision may affect other issues. This method of attack applies equally to state and local governmental bodies.

What is to be done?

Imposing limitations on terms in office merely handicaps a politician in his or her dealings with the institutional memory of the bureaucracy. If you think it easier to deal with a bureaucrat than an elected official, then you have never had to deal with the IRS. If forced to choose, we are better off taking the politician who must periodically stand for reelection.

Restructuring our government would only offer fractional improvement. A better way to deal with government is to start with the way our government and our entire political system is viewed from inside to out.

The current paradigm defines a political system composed of competing interests. Government balances the system, picking winners and losers. Government also serves as the court of last resort. All grievances must be dealt with by government if they are not addressed privately. This has led us to an activist government, ready and willing to intervene in an ever broader sphere of influence.

This particular paradigm is under severe stress. The world is shrinking as a function of the improved ability to communicate, share or exchange information, and travel. Thus, government is called upon to balance competing interests which are not wholly within its sphere of control. Also, as shown by the examples listed earlier, government can no longer easily or safely pick winners and losers, or balance competing interests. The increased interdependence of modern society makes it harder to define or even identify a winner or a loser. Increasingly, we are all winners or losers together.

Finally, it usually costs money to solve problems. Even if a problem is solved, additional problems are often created as part of the solution. Money seems always in dwindling supply, often as a consequence of previous "solutions."

A new paradigm requires that the political system be

viewed as an ecosystem. The political ecosystem is every bit as delicate as the natural ecosystem. Just as the fluttering of a hypothetical butterfly can initiate a chain reaction which results in a hail storm across the continent, so can well meaning efforts to incarcerate more criminals result in both a crime wave and a fiscal fiasco.

Each of us must put our own lives in order, taking full responsibility for all of our actions (and non-actions) and participating with knowledge and integrity in the political system. We must become members of a community who take the initiative to help each other. We must avoid the temptation to cast groups or individuals in the role of scapegoat. And, we must invoke government only sparingly.

The only way to assure that the political ecosystem stays in balance is to build that balance at the most basic level in the system: with the individual citizen.

Chapter Eleven

Change the World I:
Money, Trade & Taxation

WHEN I WAS GROWING UP in the late '60s and early '70s there was a time when Chairman Mao's so-called *Little Red Book* was very popular with my age group, and in college, I took a course in the history of the People's Republic of China, we studied the revolution led by Chairman Mao. One of the few things I remember from that course was an assigned reading entitled, "One Spark Can Start a Prairie Fire," a parable that Mao had copied from ancient Chinese philosophers.

It may be appropriate to consider here. One spark can start a fire — one person can change the world. Modern science has invented the study of chaotic systems, beginning with what is called the Lorenz Effect. James Gleick in his book *Chaos* describes this effect, wherein a butterfly's wings can set in motion events in southern California which weeks later result in a hailstorm in the northeastern states. Chairman Mao was right — one spark can start a prairie fire; one butterfly can create a hailstorm; one person can change the world.

I have a friend, Frank Callahan, who has changed our world. In 1952 he and others were confronted with a problem: how to help a small farmers' cooperative in Nebraska sell flour that no one really wanted. The people at the cooperative were stuck on the belief that the only way to sell flour was in a traditional ten pound bag. Luckily for them, Callahan was not convinced, and the result of his skepticism became Duncan Hines Cake Mix. One of the problems initially faced by Duncan Hines was women's reluctance to use "store bought" cake mix as opposed to making cakes "from scratch." After intense consumer research, Callahan and his team altered the Duncan Hines formula to remove powdered eggs and powdered milk. Now, fresh ingredients had to be added by the "in home baker," making the project of mixing a Duncan Hines cake more like baking "from scratch."

Think for a moment about the implications to the grain cooperative, its members, grocery stores, and American women, and then think about what trends either began or were encouraged by something as mundane as a cake mix. The world indeed changed.

During his marketing career, Callahan has introduced products from the Purina Company, The Gallo Brothers, Pentel Corporation, and helped make Circle K Corporation the second largest convenience store chain in the United States. It is difficult to conceive of being alive in America today without being affected by what this man has done.

There are two reasons for Callahan's high ratio of success. First, he pays attention to what is going on in his own mind and in the minds of those around him — he has his finger on the pulse of the consumer. Second, he has a discipline for thinking through a situation, setting objectives, then following through to make something happen. (Frank Callahan is just one of many who practice a disciplined approach to thinking and doing. In the last section of this book, this discipline will be described.)

Each of us, individually, is capable of changing the

world, and collectively, we can multiply our impact. Following are some recommendations about what I believe should be changed here in the United States. These recommendations are based on everything you have read so far, my experiences in life to date, and my belief system. Whether or not you agree with these suggestions, I hope you will at least think carefully about them.

ESTABLISH A VALUE FOR MONEY BASED ON THE PRINCIPLE OF FAIR EXCHANGE VALUE AND CONSISTENT WITH THE THEORIES OF ADAM SMITH, AS DEFINED IN *THE WEALTH OF NATIONS*.

In the past, money came into the economy from the Treasury. People earned money and saved it in their banks or savings and loan associations. Using the savings of their depositors, these institutions made loans. The amount any institution could loan was a function of the total deposits less a reserve amount sufficient to meet any depositor's desire to withdraw money. The system no longer works in this manner.

Now, when a consumer borrows money to buy a house or car, or pays for lunch with a bank card, the financial institution sells these loans. Loans of a given kind, home mortgages for example, are bundled and sold as a group to investors. When these loans are sold, their value is somewhat discounted; the financial institution receives a portion of the interest income to be generated over the life of the loan, as well as the principle. As the borrower makes loan payments to the financial institution, these payments are paid in turn to the investor. In this manner, the financial institution has become an agent for investors, many of whom are located overseas, or are themselves large institutions such as pension funds or insurance companies.

The result is the creation of an artificial economy that makes more money available than ever before, but it is borrowed money rather than earned. What happens when foreign and institutional investors either choose to stop or are forced to stop purchasing these debt securities? How will Americans buy their new cars, stereos, major appliances, or homes?

This day will inevitably come. The recent declines in the Japanese securities market, along with scandals in Japan which have shaken the confidence of that country's investors in their markets, have wiped out over one-third of the value of the Japanese stock exchange. These securities are the source of much of the wealth that Japanese institutions have used to purchase American government and financial institution debt instruments. Consequently, sales of stocks, bonds, and debt securities to Japan have slowed and continue to drop steadily. The American standard of living depends on debt, as opposed to earned income, and with debt ever harder to obtain that standard has already begun to decline.

Before 1960 Americans saved and avoided debt. Beginning with the financial stress caused by the Viet Nam war, continuing with the oil shocks of the '70s, and culminating with the use of debt as a security in the '80s, the American economy has been subjected to significant inflationary pressure. During the early 1900s, a safety valve was added to the American economic system to avoid the very problems the system is currently experiencing. That safety valve was the creation of the Federal Reserve Board.

The Federal Reserve Board is supposed to control the growth of the money supply, holding it to no more than three to five percent per annum. Before 1971 this growth in the money supply was tied to the supply of gold. The pressures of Viet Nam and the lack of government discipline made the gold standard untenable, and since 1971 the size of the money supply has had no relation to any objective standard. As a consequence, over the last twenty years the increase in the money supply has seldom been less than five percent annually (the supposed upper limit), and has often risen in excess of ten percent. Vast hoards of dollars are held by the Europeans, the Japanese, and others and have been used to finance American individual and government debt. There are simply too many dollars and too much debt. The Federal Reserve Board has not done its job — the American dollar has effectively been debased and devalued.

Virtually every expert recognizes that this is a problem, but no one is sure where it will lead. The only rational assumption is that the Federal Reserve Board will continue to behave as it has over the past three decades, continuing the unwarranted inflationary expansion of the money supply. If this assumption is correct, it makes no sense for Americans to save their money. Due to the actions of the Federal Reserve Board, the dollar you deposit in your savings account today will be worth 90 cents next year, or ten percent less, while the interest earned on that dollar will seldom exceed six or eight percent. If the effect of price inflation is added to this effect of the Federal Reserve Board's ill-advised growth in money supply policy, those people who save money become even worse off.

Since Americans are not saving money, and foreign/ institutional investors are less willing to finance U.S. government and consumer debt, it is obvious that we will no longer be able to increase debt to finance our government and our lifestyle. What then is the solution?

We must put our economy back into balance, stop the reliance on tax transfers, debt, and inflated money as substitutes for earned income, and cease giving our markets, property, and securities away to foreign competitors. In other words, we must begin to act in our own enlightened self-interest.

In *The Fatal Conceit*, F. A. Hayek says the following about money: "Though an indispensible requirement for the functioning of an extensive order of cooperation of free people, money has almost from its first appearance been so shamelessly abused by governments that it has become the prime source of disturbance of all self-ordering processes in the extended order of human cooperation. The history of government management of money has, except for a few short happy periods, been one of incessant fraud and deception."

The Federal Reserve Board must no longer be allowed the discretion to determine the growth of the U.S. money supply on the basis of expediency. The value of raw materials including associated labor produced each year (using Smith's natural price or Peek's "fair exchange value" price to measure the value) should determine how much the money supply is allowed to grow. Thus, we as Americans will be able to earn the money we need to live, rather than going into debt as either a hedge against inflation or to finance or borrow the money to enjoy our lifestyle.

In accomplishing this, the proposed National Economic Stability Act (NESA) should be enacted to create balance in our economy. The provisions of the Act are included as Appendix C to this book. NESA has been developed by the National Organization for Raw Materials and is described in *Raw Materials Economics* by Charles Walters Jr.

The result of this change is a sound economy — the firm foundation from which all of the other ills of society can be addressed. Without building a sound economic base which rests on creating an earned income in balance with the principal of "fair exchange value," any other change we make will be no more than spitting into the wind.

The first step is for each of us to begin living our lives in a manner consistent with sound economic principles. These are described in detail in Chapter Seventeen, entitled "Charity Begins At Home."

Next, each of us can begin to pressure Congress to live up to the requirements set forth in Section 8 of the United States Constitution, which regulates the value of money. (See Appendix D for text of the Constitution and Bill of Rights.) The value of our money should be based upon a raw material standard, as described above. The dollars in circulation should be valued so they represent their proportionate share of the raw materials produced from nature. When accomplished, this will result in the price of a bushel of wheat being in the range of ten dollars, relative to 1991 dollars. Other raw materials will be similarly affected.

This will raise prices to consumers, but prices will be offset by other positive effects. First, billions of dollars in subsidies, tax breaks, low interest loans, and price supports will become unnecessary. So will the people who administer these programs, who can then begin to do something "productive" with their lives. Second, farmers and other producers of raw materials will spend new money on goods and services. In turn, this will result in more dollars being spent on down the line. Rather than borrow, print, or tax money to sustain a lifestyle, Americans will actually start to earn money to pay for what they consume. The specific techniques enabling us to convince Congress to do what must be done will be discussed in detail in the chapter entitled, "Our Quality of Life."

ESTABLISH A FOREIGN TRADE POLICY BASED ON
FAIR EXCHANGE VALUE.

Free trade is a fiasco — read Kevin Phillips for the
proof. America has opened its borders to virtually any
product at any price. In order to compete, American companies have moved millions of jobs overseas. Additional American jobs have been lost to foreign companies who have often
used predatory pricings to destroy their American competitors
and gain market share. They then sit back, use cheap labor to
produce products at less than "fair exchange value" rates,
and reap the rewards. Free trade has become a free ride for
our foreign competitors.

Charles Walters, in his book *Unforgiven*, writes that
establishing parity (referring to fair exchange value) for raw
materials "would secure parity for labor by bringing into
focus the problems of the import invasion." He says that
cheap goods which flow to the U.S. have the same effect as
importing cheap labor here to replace the American labor
force. Parity in raw materials would oblige the government
to set tariffs on imports to ensure that they "enter the United
States trade channels on par with goods produced at the
American wage scale." In this scheme, parity and structural
balance "must govern all sectors of the American economy,
labor included, if full employment and a secure food lifeline
are to be maintained."

Conditions here deteriorated so much that by 1986 the
United States and its trading partners were forced to take
action to slow the flood of imports and forestall the collapse
of American manufacturing: they depressed the dollar's
exchange rate by 30 to 40 percent relative to other currencies. Manufacturing did not collapse, but it still continues to
decline. The depressed dollar artificially created low prices

in terms of U.S. products, property, stocks, and bonds. The resulting fire sale has turned the United States into a bargain basement where companies, real estate, and natural resources are snapped up by foreign investors.

The United States became so relatively cheap that foreign companies rushed in to set up manufacturing plants (called "transplants") throughout those areas of the U.S. where organized labor is weakest. Unfortunately, even if the free trade fiasco is remedied, these companies will still maintain their American transplants in the United States, which will enable them to avoid most of the negative impact of a corrective tariff. Top management, financing, suppliers, and profits from the transplants will not come from or remain in the United States.

The President and Congress must be pressured to replace free trade with a policy of fair trade. Fair trade would dictate an automatic reciprocal treatment for our trading partners keyed to the "fair exchange value" principle. In other words, we would finally compare apples to apples.

There exist several models of how fair trade can and should work. One is that employed by Japan. Why are the Japanese so resistant about importing steel, autos, or cheap food, such as American rice or beef, into their country? Why do the Japanese sell their entertainment systems here in the United States for less than half they charge in Tokyo? Why will the Japanese not allow the free flow of imported autos into their country? The same questions can be as easily asked about the countries of Western Europe. The answer is that these economies all operate wisely within their borders on the principle of "fair exchange value." Why are we not doing likewise?

This is not to suggest that a fair trade policy should, or even could, be used to address competitive issues such as quality, quantity, or design. Fair trade will only work if it equalizes the relative economic strengths of separate economies, so that goods priced in one economy on the basis of "fair exchange value" can be priced in a different economy on an equivalent basis.

To appreciate this policy imagine a canal along a river. Locks in the canal make it possible to navigate the river, but do not allow any more or less water to flow through it. The water still originates in small streams, travels down the river, reaches the sea, evaporates, rains over land, and collects again in the small streams. The cycle repeats itself and balance is maintained.

Economies which operate on the basis of "fair exchange value" follow the same principles as the cycle of water in nature and the canal. Trade between nations can be equalized using a tariff. Once a tariff is collected on apples moving from Nation A to Nation B, that tariff should be held on deposit in Nation B. Nation A then has a credit which it can use to purchase bananas from Nation B at a discount. In effect, we will have created a system, similar to the locks in a canal, which can be used as a "barter bank" to equalize different economic systems — each of which functions in balance with a "fair exchange value" unique to its circumstances. Using tariffs not as a balancing mechanism, but to gain competitive advantage, as do the Japanese, perverts the concept.

As a final note, Dr. Thomas Boyd, president of Lambuth University in Tennessee, points out that the measures suggested above will only eliminate unfair trading practices while doing little to prepare America to become a better world competitor. He says, "One of the great stumbling blocks in our way to becoming effective competitors is the 1977 Corrupt Practices Act which holds American business overseas to a standard of conduct equivalent to what is expected of Americans trading at home." Besides failing to account for cultural differences around the world, "the vague provisions of the Act, along with harsh penalties for failure to comply with the Act, intimidate American business people overseas. Consequently, they do nothing that would create even an appearance of impropriety." The results, according to Boyd, are lost sales, lost market share, lost profits, and lost jobs.

The Corrupt Practices Act must be repealed, and further improvement of American competitiveness abroad must begin at home. Boyd believes the American government should focus its domestic efforts toward "utilization of tax and investment credit to encourage reformation of capital." In his opinion, the domestic agenda also shows "need for an incentive program to completely redesign and rebuild the productive infrastructure of the country. We're going the wrong way as a nation when usable railroad track has dropped from 198,000 miles to 137,000 miles over the past ten years."

ABOLISH THE FEDERAL INCOME TAX, REPLACING IT WITH A NATIONAL GRADUATED SALES TAX AND A BALANCED BUDGET AMENDMENT TO THE CONSTITUTION.

Our current tax system which relies mainly on the income tax at the federal and state level is misguided, unproductive, and all too often abusive to the taxpayers. The income tax encourages spending rather than saving, and it encourages people to cheat, hide income, and pad expenses to reduce their tax liability. It fails to collect taxes from vast sectors of the economy (such as drug dealers), unfairly increasing the burden on law abiding, productive members of society. The income tax collection process has spawned a costly public and private bureaucracy which produces little of value to society, wasting billions of dollars and millions of hours of what could be productive time. Income tax audit procedures presume citizens to be guilty until proven innocent, violating traditional American notions of fair play and justice. Income tax regulations have become so arcane and confusing, the small taxpayer cannot afford competent professional help with tax planning and preparation, or the time to learn the rules well enough to protect his or her interests. This results in small taxpayers paying more than necessary, or more than they perceive to be necessary. The income tax withholding system takes billions of dollars from the taxpayers of America, holds those dollars for more than a year in some cases, and makes life more difficult for millions of Americans who can least afford its added burdens.

All of these factors have increasingly alienated Americans from their government at all levels. Cynicism, anger, and even violence have resulted. Most Americans assume the system is basically unfair. Income tax has helped to create an adversarial relationship between the government and its citizens.

I propose the abolition of all federal, state, and local corporate and individual income taxes, to be replaced by a system of sales and value-added taxes. Accomplished by repealing the 16th Amendment of the Constitution (see Appendix D), abolition of income taxes would also make possible the termination of at least 50 percent of the bureaucrats who enforce collection of these taxes.

Obviously, government cannot just stop or cease to exist — government is in many respects necessary and helpful. Its operation should be funded by another means of generating revenue: a graduated sales tax. The sales tax would be limited, so that no more than 30 percent of the gross national product produced in the United States could be collected through this mechanism to support all levels of government. Subsistence items (food, non-luxury clothing, rents, and non-luxury housing) would be exempt from any tax. The sales tax would be set at a variable rate, with basic goods and services at the lowest rates and luxury goods and services taxed at the highest rates. Creation of a temporary sales tax surcharge calculated to raise an additional 2.5 percent of gross national product could be collected for the express purpose of retiring the principal of the national debt. When the debt is paid off this additional tax surcharge would expire.

All sales tax revenues would be collected using the existing machinery at the local city and county level. This avoids duplication of effort and waste, making possible the earlier proposed reduction in the staff size of the Internal Revenue Service. Congress would be expected to mandate a fair mechanism for splitting revenue with other subdivisions of government; failure to do so could jeopardize our existing social contract.

Finally, government expenditures should be prohibited by a Constitutional Amendment from exceeding collections, assuring a balanced operating budget. Debt would only be permitted in case of war or national emergency declared by a two-thirds vote of both Houses of Congress.

Virtually every disadvantage of the current system of income taxation is addressed with the proposal above; further, the sales tax approach will encourage savings, eliminate bureaucracy, and simplify government.

Chapter Twelve

Change the World II:
Drug Abuse, Social Services, Health, Education & Welfare

REQUIRE TWO YEARS OF PUBLIC SERVICE FROM ALL AMERICANS.

The draft is now a part of history; with its passing we have lost a tradition of public service, which may not prove to be a good thing in the long run. Many of the problems confronting the United States relate to people, relationships, and alienation. These problems are human in scope and require human caring, attention, and time before they can be solved. The old solution of throwing money at problems and creating new bureaucracies has been shown not to work. Something else should be tried: people power.

Our out of balance economy, coupled with misguided government aid programs aimed at poor people, have had an unfortunate and unforeseen side effect — the disintegration of the family. Young people do not have enough positive adult role models. Adults cannot or will not take the time to give youngsters the personal individual attention required to prepare those youngsters to become successful, productive members of society. Old people vegetate in nursing homes cut off from family and friends, becoming expensive burdens. All of these could benefit from people power.

People power could make headway on other fronts, as well. Our nation's infrastructure suffers from deferred maintenance, much of which could be provided by individuals as part of a public service program. Significant environmental damage could be repaired, and conservation initiatives launched by these same people. Other people filling their public service requirement could help teachers work with children suffering from learning problems. The list of areas where people power can make a sure difference is endless.

Two years of public service should become an obligation which applies to anyone who has not yet given two years of service to the military, Peace Corps, VISTA, or the like. This public service requirement could be met on any basis that is convenient for the individual, and the organization he or she chooses to help. The individual could commit two years all at once, or one month, week, or day at a time. People who complete the service requirement would become eligible for a two-year scholarship program to the college of their choice, which would be fully transferable to other members of their family. A second benefit would be the earned ability to participate in the Veterans' Administration Home Mortgage program. Completion of the public service requirement would be left to the individual and tracked by the Social Security Administration. There would be no penalty imposed by government for failure to complete this public service. Non-participation would be an individual choice.

In addition to the obvious physical and human benefits this program would provide to other citizens and the nation as a whole, there is an additional significant "plus" for this program. Americans will learn that there is no free ride. The point will be made that American citizenship carries with it the obligation or responsibility to give something back, contribute to the general improvement of the country and its people, and actively make a difference. Why be satisfied with a "Thousand Points of Light", when we can create 250 million points of light? We can bring Americans closer together in this way and create a national sense of community.

EXPAND JURISDICTION OF THE BUREAU OF ALCO-HOL, TOBACCO, AND FIREARMS TO ENCOMPASS ALL CONTROLLED SUBSTANCES, ELIMINATE CRIMINAL PENALTIES FOR SALE AND USE OF CON-TROLLED SUBSTANCES, AND ABOLISH THE DRUG ENFORCEMENT ADMINISTRATION.

The "War on Drugs" is lost. It was as inappropriate a war to wage as any in our history. Why do we choose to ban some drugs and not others? Tobacco is more dangerous and more addictive than cocaine. Alcohol is no better, and perhaps worse in many ways, than marijuana. The people with the most to gain from our current drug policy are the "Drug Lords." These people become rich as they sell drugs at artificially inflated prices. They can maintain exorbitantly high prices because of substance scarcity imposed by the government's only partially effective interdiction efforts. The result is a black market economy exempt from taxation involving billions of dollars every year, which corrupts all levels of society from school children to international bankers. The drug trade is a good example of a raw material priced out of balance in the opposite direction, with respect to the principle of "fair exchange value." The resulting lack of natural balance from overpricing (rather than underpricing) perverts the entire economy just as badly.

The other people with the most to gain from our current drug policies are the politicians, who use fear of drugs to gain office, and the bureaucrats and law enforcement agencies who manage budgets that have been bloated to build the empires that fight mostly losing battles. Other winners include the people who investigate, litigate, and then incarcerate the countless low-level pawns caught up in this "war."

Those of us with the most to lose are bystanders to the direct action. We are the ones who pick up the pieces of our children's lives after they are destroyed or damaged by drugs. We are the ones who pay the taxes; our money finances the high-tech tools of the law enforcement trade, pays the costs of the legal system and its accoutrements, then operates the countless jails needed to accommodate the war's casualties. Incredibly important human and economic resources are wasted fighting our "War on Drugs."

A disturbing call for the suspension of Constitutional rights to grant police the freedom to conduct random searches was recently made by Chicago Police Superintendent LeRoy Martin. He had recently completed a trip to the People's Republic of China, where he found "there are some things they do that are better than we do." According to Martin, our communities are under siege, "and police find themselves helpless because of civil rights." Martin is concerned that police are unduly hampered from adequately fighting crime. This would indicate the people and the police (government) are being forced into an adversarial relationship which could become fatal to our basic freedoms.

This is not an argument for drug use or tolerance. The use of controlled substances is not advocated, nor should criminals be coddled. Neither is this a gripe with law enforcement and other public safety officers. On the contrary, we cannot continue to waste these brave men and women, or the resources involved in enforcing what is an obviously irrational

107

policy. As Peter F. Drucker suggests in *The New Realities*, "it might be more productive then to do the one thing we can do: take the profits out of the traffic in drugs by eliminating criminal penalties on drug use — 'immoral' though this sounds."

The current policy to eradicate drug use is based on a double standard which makes it acceptable for me to drink beer and smoke cigarettes, but sends you to jail for using other similar, mood-altering substances. We must tear down the barriers which spring up between government and its citizens, when government attempts to control behavior which most people believe cannot or will not be controlled, and which we generally believe to be most dangerous to those people who engage in the behavior, not to the rest of us.

Henry Grady Weaver in *The Mainspring of Human Progress* said, "Human energy cannot operate effectively except when men are free to act and to be responsible for their actions. But liberty does not mean license; for no one has a right to infringe upon the rights of others." As Weaver explained, we have both legal restraints and moral restraints on our behavior, "but laws on the statute books can never be an adequate substitute for moral restraint based on enlightened self-interest — which means a recognition of one's duties as well as of one's rights." He believes that extending laws into areas where they cannot be enforced does more harm than good for it makes the legal system a substitute for individual morality and it increases government's role without ensuring citizens' lawful behavior. "Any attempt to give the government the responsibilities which properly belong to the individual citizens works at cross-purposes to the advancement of personal freedom."

Following these lines of reasoning, all drugs should be regulated and taxed, by expanding the jurisdiction of the existing Bureau of Alcohol, Tobacco, and Firearms to administer the policy. Education, peer pressure, social/medical institutions, and family/church institutions are available and can be effective in preventing abuse. We must heal the drug disease, rather than wage a war of attrition. Beating the people of America into a state of submission is more appropriate to a totalitarian government than to our democracy.

LEARN BY DOING; DISNEYLAND IN THE CLASS-ROOM; LEARNING IS FUN.

Because I grew up on a small ranch that required the efforts of our entire family to operate, I have a first-hand understanding of the importance of learning by doing. All the books in the world cannot teach a person how to ride a horse, one only learns by doing it. Like most people, I did not realize the things I was learning as a child, or even that I was learning things; learning was a natural part of daily life.

My school experiences frequently showed me the other side of education and learning — that of boredom. Teachers are expected to stand in front of a room full of children and lecture, but lectures bore the better students and are lost on the slower learners. As teacher pay and benefits fall farther behind the market, fewer and less-qualified people choose teaching as a profession. As classes grow larger in response to our economic crises, individual attention becomes more scarce. Children become bored, and to alleviate the boredom, many become discipline problems, drop out (mentally first, then physically), and end up as burdens on society.

One solution is offered by a man named Jack Taub. Taub, former CEO and majority shareholder of an information service called The Source, is currently building something he calls the Community Learning Network. Taub himself dropped out of school at an early age because of boredom. To address the boredom problem, he has created a potential system that he says, "will make going to school like going to Disneyland."

The Taub system uses satellites, computers, and television to give every student in every classroom in every school access to all of the information that is currently published. Instead of buying information such as computer programs, films, and games, the school systems can rent it for a nominal fee. Taub has designed the software to link together almost any computer hardware a school system might own, so nothing previously purchased needs to be wasted. Parents can access the system from home to see how their children are doing. Electronic mail, school administrative systems, and all of the other bells and whistles are included in the package.

The net effect of Taub's system is that each child can enjoy individual teacher attention, individualized lesson plans, specialized reading and research assignments, easy parent involvement, and can learn at his or her own speed. Teachers can spend less time lecturing and more time with hands-on learning in Taub's system. Students ought to learn more. And, in initial tests, the cost of Taub's Community Learning Network is within existing financial limits of school systems. If he succeeds, Jack Taub will ban boredom from the classroom.

Whether or not this particular approach catches on, a system like this would allow one child to read Shakespeare, while another watches a movie of the same play. It would allow teachers to customize each student's lesson plan by capitalizing on his or her natural strengths or weaknesses, and it would involve the parents. This approach is, at a minimum, what our educational system needs.

We also need to better compensate our teachers, and programs that have proved useful in other professions, such as the team approach, should be tried in education. For example, teachers could be placed at the top of a pyramid consisting of a team of professional educators, para-professionals, student teachers, and parents. This team could work together to get the most out of each lesson for each child. A concept of "master teacher," the teacher qualified to be the team leader, would make possible a compensation system that creates a career path for advancement within the classroom. This would end the practice of kicking the most capable teachers upstairs into administration so they can earn a living.

Fred Heunfeld, former president of the National Organization or Raw Materials (NORM) points out that our school system seems to be "structured to teach our children to think they're learning, when in reality our educators ought to enable our children to learn to think." In this regard, the "learn by doing" approach should be encouraged. The 4-H and the Girl and Boy Scouts all do this quite well. With the shift away from a lecture-based system of teaching to the customized, computer-assisted team approach, "learn by doing" becomes a realistic system for our primary and secondary schools, colleges and universities. Best of all, it should take no more, and possibly less, than we currently spend on education.

Finally, no opportunity for innovation in education should be ignored. This includes allowing private enterprise to compete with the entrenched educational systems to provide a "choice" for parents. The objective of education is to educate our children, not maintain an existing system. Where market forces can be brought into play, those forces will ultimately improve the range of options and the quality of the product delivered to our children.

BECOME RESPONSIBLE FOR YOUR HEALTH, SEIZE
THE SYSTEM, AND MAKE IT WORK.

Our current crisis in the health industry is the direct
consequence of years of greed, fear, and ignorance. Each of
us helped make this reality, now each of us must deal with
the results of our neglect.

The place to start is with ourselves. Take control of
your health. Eat right, exercise a little every day. Do not
poison your body with alcohol, tobacco, and the other
controlled substances. Structure your life to avoid stress.
Have more fun in what you do. Laugh regularly.

The foregoing is Dr. Mike's prescription for a long and
happy life. No one should be surprised with that advice. We
all know how to take care of ourselves, but surprisingly few
of us do it. I confess that in this I must ask you to do as I
say, not as I do! Nevertheless, within the last several months
I have begun to take conscious control of my own health
and so should you. While we are getting our lives in order,
consider the following.

Our entire health system begins with the implicit assumption that each of us is looking to get sick. We fear the
effects of illness, so we buy insurance. Spending money,
and betting against ourselves, an entire industry has sprung
up to cater to our fears. Now, over 37 million of us cannot
afford to place that bet, and our fear multiplies.

Meanwhile, back at the hospital, we have structured a
delivery system guaranteed to maximize cost. We do not
allow many people to become doctors, so those that make it
through the system have a license to charge an arm and a leg
for their services. Because they make so much money,
doctors have come to be expected by their patients and
society to live up to unrealistic expectations of infallibility.

Because they make so much (and thus have deep pockets) and usually work for very large institutions (with even deeper pockets), doctors and hospitals have become targets for another greedy bunch — the lawyers.

Every doctor knows he or she will eventually become a defendant in a malpractice action. Fear of this on the part of the doctors, fueled by their greed, by society's unrealistically high expectations, by the greed of patients and the greed of their lawyers, has created the malpractice insurance industry and the resulting malpractice crisis in medical care.

The net effect of all of this is to drive up the cost of medical care. Doctors frequently order unnecessary tests, and in general practice defensive medicine to protect themselves from the inevitable law suit. Hospitals rush to buy all the latest equipment in order to assure that these tests can be conducted, as well as to attract doctors and assure themselves high patient counts. It is an upward spiral with no end in sight. Eventually, somebody has to pay for it, and as usual, it is you and me.

One method the medical community relies on to cover these costs is to perform unnecessary surgeries, such as hysterectomies or insertion of pacemakers, which help to maintain cash flow. The inescapable result of this is more litigation. Another method is "cost shifting," mentioned earlier, which is charging the shortfall in hospital costs to the paying customers (those with insurance). For years, the favorite cost shifting targets were Medicare and Medicaid patients, until federal officials got smart and refused to pay more than their fair share. Now, insurance companies, employees, and patients in private rooms feel the pinch of "cost shifting." Still, hospitals remain on the brink of bankruptcy, even after charging several dollars for a toothbrush or an aspirin tablet.

113

Another piece of the puzzle is drugs. The costs to develop a new drug are so high, and the regulatory approval process so long, that many drug companies tend to maximize the return on their products beyond all reason. Using the research approval cycle as an excuse, companies develop brand name drugs which are pushed to doctors, pharmacies, and hospitals by aggressive marketing and sales organizations, at prices two or three times the price of the same drug with a generic label.

Long term care also contributes to the financial and ethical crises confronting medicine and society. The demise of the extended family has created a new industry. Older people are written off and warehoused in nursing homes, where their care often fails to meet the minimum standards necessary to maintain health or dignity.

Extreme measures are undertaken to save lives or keep terminally ill patients alive longer. These measures are very expensive and the quality of life experienced by the patients upon whom these treatments are inflicted is usually marginal, or worse.

Taken together, all of these factors contribute to a national health care system that costs more and delivers less than it should. The crisis in American medicine has been much written about, and many competing solutions have been offered. No decision has been made yet to solve the crisis, however, nor has a consensus been reached about how to reach such a decision. The President and/or Congress will probably attempt to delay any meaningful discussion about what to do until after the 1992 election.

Regardless of what the national government does about the problem, there are several specific actions we can take to deal with the underlying causes of this crisis: the greed, fear and ignorance. The objective is to alter the consciousness of the people who must eventually decide how to deal with the problem.

First, make an appointment with your doctor. Make it late in the day, so the two of you can talk without feeling pressured by the next appointment. Discuss this issue with him or her. Explain the points just made and ask for his or her comments. Learn all you can. Ask what he or she is personally doing to break the cycle of greed, fear, and ignorance. Ask the same question regarding the local medical society. Put your doctor on the spot. Let it be known that he or she shares personal responsibility for what is wrong with the system. How much time does he or she spend caring for those who cannot afford medical care? This will probably prove an uncomfortable subject for the doctor, but it is time that America's medical professionals were confronted with these issues in real, personal, human terms. The most realistic concern should be that of the patient, who the doctor depends upon for his or her livelihood, and that is you.

Next, repeat the process two more times. Go see your attorney if you have one, even if he or she does not make a living from personal injury litigation, and have the same conversation. Repeat the process again with your insurance agent. When talking to your insurance agent, take advantage of his or her knowledge of the system. Of all the people involved in delivering and financing medical care in the United States, your insurance agent is the person who has most in common with you, and who is most likely to give you an accurate picture of what is really going on and why.

After that, bring all three of these people together in one place and exchange ideas. The objective of this meeting is to identify problems and brainstorm solutions. After you read Chapter Eighteen, "Our Quality of Life," you will have a better idea about how to conduct this meeting. The point of all of this is to bring the problem to a personal level and focus on personal actions that each of us can take. Together we can make some improvements. These solutions will reveal themselves to us if we have the courage to look for them, and are willing to invest the time.

What would happen if 100,000 doctors, lawyers, and insurance agents were forced by patients to confront their own painfully personal responsibility for the medical crisis in the United States? My bet is, the system would change for the better.

Now it is possible to really make a difference. Go to see three other people and, if possible, take your doctor, lawyer, and insurance agent with you. These people are your Representative in the United States Senate or House (your choice), a local politician at the city or county level, and either the person responsible for managing your company's health program or the administrator of your local hospital. Put them on the spot. Let them know you are fed up with the system and tired of lame explanations about why they cannot deal with the problem. Demand action — NOW! Finally, write every one of these six people once a month and ask them what they have done during the past four weeks to deal with the issues.

All of this no doubt sounds like a lot of work, and it is. But what is outlined above is a campaign of pressure to make those people who really are responsible for the crisis face that responsibility, accept it, and begin to act to change it. Enough of this pressure will force action.

During all these conversations, meetings, and correspondence, bring up the following discussion points:

1. Consider that the basic problem confronting medicine is a violation of Adam Smith's law of supply and

demand. The commodity in short supply is the doctor. So, instead of having a few doctors who will charge exorbitant rates, why not increase the supply of doctors in society over the next ten or fifteen years by 30 to 50 percent?

2. Consider that doctors have evolved a monopoly on delivery of professional advice, but not on the possession of professional knowledge. There are other (many other) health care providers who can deliver medical care. Perhaps it is time to dramatically expand the number of nurse-practitioners and para-medics, as well as their ability to operate within the system to deliver lower-cost health care. Perhaps it is time to break the monopoly.

3. Consider that the main reason neither of the foregoing is possible at this time is that all parties suffer from fear of litigation. Perhaps it is time to change the way lawyers do business with respect to medical malpractice, by eliminating the concept of punitive damages and mandating a system not unlike Workers' Compensation to deal with mistakes made by medical professionals. Perhaps the emphasis of our legal system should be less concerned with blaming and punishing, and more concerned with alleviating the on-going pain and suffering.

4. Consider that one of the reasons costs can escalate so quickly is that no one is really responsible for holding them down.

The largest customer for medical services in this country is the federal government. If all federal programs were combined into one, and Congress were to mandate that spending for those programs shall increase at a level no greater than that necessary to account for inflation and the increased numbers of qualifying people, there would be a major impact on escalating expenditures. If insurance companies and other customers agree to hold that same line, then doctors and hospitals would find themselves between a rock and a hard spot. The system would change, and to our benefit.

According to Adam Smith in *The Wealth of Nations,* a monopolistic price is the one which is "upon every occasion the highest which can be squeezed out of the buyers, or which, it is supposed, they will consent to give." The natural price, based on free competition is "the lowest which the sellers can commonly afford to take, and at the same time continue their business." The American Medical Association has created an effective monopoly on the delivery of health care. It has done a very good job of restricting the number of doctors allowed to practice medicine in this country, relying on long educational programs, testing, and the great expense of becoming a doctor.

The key to solving the health crisis in this country and around the world is to make it easier to practice medicine. First, we need to make it easier to become a doctor. Then, we need to change the system of adjudicating disputes between doctors and patients, to eliminate the incredible climate of fear pervading the medical institutions of our country.

If you are a doctor or a lawyer you most likely disagree with everything said here. Nevertheless, please seriously consider the best interests of your community, as opposed to your pocketbook. Doctors and lawyers should not have to take vows of poverty. They should, however, think about how much the market can bear before it is destroyed by their actions. Reread the oath you took upon becoming a doctor and ask yourself if your pricing policies perhaps violate a portion of that oath.

The program outlined above is only the minimum; the maximum is limited by nothing but imagination and will.

Many may scoff at this program, considering it naive and unrealistic, and convinced there is too much inertia in the current system for it to be changed. If that is how you feel, look at the history of just one group, Mothers Against Drunk Driving (MADD), and the woman who founded MADD. This group has succeeded in changing the attitude of an entire nation with respect to alcohol consumption. One person, alone, can make a difference. You or I can be that person if we have the guts to believe in ourselves. Remember the cake mix. We can change the world if we dare.

WIN THE WAR ON POVERTY USING EARNED INCOME, NOT WELFARE.

The social welfare system in America is the fastest growing, most wasteful portion of the federal budget. People receiving assistance comprise a larger and larger portion of the population, while more and more families are becoming homeless and being forced to live on the streets. Why? Because these people are falling between the cracks as society relies ever more heavily on debt and the dole rather than earned income to operate.

We will always need to provide for the mentally, socially, and economically handicapped. However, the current situation involving billions of dollars and millions of people makes every one of us, from the taxpayer to the recipient, a loser.

A balanced economy based on earned income, a rational fair trade policy based on reciprocity, and money with a stable value will address the current crises of welfare, homelessness, and crime by providing *real* jobs, *real* opportunity, and dignity to most of those members of our society living on the margins.

119

The current system insults both the dignity and intelligence of the recipients, forcing them into a posture of subservience to a faceless bureaucracy which literally holds, and too often arbitrarily exercises, the power of life and death over these unfortunates. Central planning, government decision making and miserly benefits are poor substitutes for productive private sector jobs and individual financial independence. The way to deal with our growing problems of an emerging welfare class is to implement the program defined in Chapter Eleven to bring the economy back into balance, thus creating *real* opportunity. Then, our welfare system will once again assume its proper role of helping those who truly need help rather than continuing to serve as a human warehouse for the unemployed.

Chapter Thirteen

Change The World III:
Government & Politics

REDUCE THE SIZE OF GOVERNMENT BY TEN PERCENT OVER TEN YEARS, REVITALIZE THE FEDERAL GOVERNMENT, AND REDEDICATE THE GOVERNMENT TO ITS MISSION.

Government is a service organization designed to help productive members of society produce more effectively, by doing some things they could not otherwise do for themselves. Government does not itself produce or create value.

Adam Smith in *The Wealth of Nations* said, "There is one sort of labor which adds to the value of the subject on which it is bestowed; there is another which has no such effect. The former, as it produces a value, may be productive; the latter, unproductive." He goes on to characterize unproductive labor as that which provides a country its protection, security, and defense, although "the effect of their labor this year will not purchase its protection, security, and defense for the year to come." Speaking of those who do unproductive labor, Smith adds, "the work of all of them perishes at the very instant of its production."

Smith warned that, "Great nations are never impoverished by private, [but] they sometimes are by public illegality and misconduct." As it happens, he was warning people two hundred years ago of what has come to pass with

America. The numbers of unproductive workers may so increase, and consume so much of the country's revenue, he said, "that all the frugality and good conduct of individuals may not be able to compensate the waste and degradation of produce occasioned by this violent and enforced encroachment." To restate it, no matter what solutions we, as citizens, devise to bail our country out of its economic calamity, the solutions will fail unless we begin to minimize the drain on revenues that our overstaffed, "unproductive" government causes. We cannot afford our government any longer.

The last ten years have been a disaster for this country. Hoping that the very people who caused the problems will somehow find a solution and come to their senses is not a rational approach. In the situation we find ourselves, people are either part of the problem or part of the solution. Unfortunately, if a person is involved in making decisions for government or serving in a government position, he or she is more than likely to be part of the problem than a part of the solution. Those of us outside of government, who are not without our own problems, to be sure, are most likely to be the source of the solution.

The mission of government is defined by the United States Constitution in its Preamble: "We the people of the United States, in order to form a more perfect Union, establish justice, insure domestic tranquility, provide for the common defense, promote the general welfare, and secure the blessings of liberty to ourselves and our posterity, do ordain and establish this Constitution for the United States of America."

That's it. No more, no less. Soon after the creation of the U.S. Constitution, a Bill of Rights was added to limit the power of the government, and from time to time other amendments to the Constitution have been considered and occasionally accepted. If you have not read the Constitution and Bill of Rights since school days, turn to Appendix D— it will be worth your time.

Now, two hundred years later, as we are witnessing the demise of Communism as the only major governmental alternative, it is generally accepted that the United States has developed as good a system of government as has ever been tried. The point is that now we have too much of a good thing, and what we have can be improved.

Once hired by the government an employee with marginal, if any, competence holds a Civil Service job virtually for life, and is included in a retirement and benefit system that is no longer workable. Both of these elements, Civil Service protection and the retirement system, came into being during a different era and economic situation. In those days government workers were grossly underpaid, and good people were hard to attract. Political patronage made government a chancy profession — job security usually lasted only through the next election. So, in the spirit of reform and fairness, the Civil Service and retirement systems were created.

They are now outdated and in need of an overhaul. The solution is not to suggest some draconian quick-fix like the abolition of the Civil Service system. Together with the retirement mess, these are really symptoms of deeper problems. Additional symptoms are easy to see. Government employees have come to view themselves as "entitled" to their positions and perks. Those who deal with the public are increasingly surly and inefficient. The concept of customer or public service is too often unknown, if not rejected by our government employees. The quality of work is also slipping — documents that can make, or break, a life or a company are routinely lost.

It is not that the people employed by government cannot do their jobs. In a natural disaster or an emergency, the government usually comes through. The same agency that spends $600 for toilet seats did an admirable job in Kuwait when the chips were down.

But, in the day-to-day grind of business as usual, there is no spirit or dedication readily visible to the casual observer. We are all accustomed to being treated shoddily. Anyone who has to deal with government must be prepared to spend much of life on hold, just waiting.

Two years ago I was involved in the purchase of a company. The company we bought participated in a Small Business Administration program designed to help minority-owned companies. Because our purchase changed the ownership to such a degree that our eligibility for the program ended, we went to the SBA to ask how to handle the orderly termination of the company from their program. After waiting more than six weeks, we were finally granted an appointment. The meeting began an hour late and lasted longer than two hours. The three SBA officials meeting with us wandered in and out of the meeting, asking the same questions over and over again, and were never able to answer our question. My solution for this type of management and treatment is to suggest a process of reduction, redefinition, and rededication.

First, reduction. The size of government should be reduced by ten percent over the next ten years. We should not be willing to accept the old ploy of merely reducing the size of the rate of growth which is generally what is meant by reduction when government uses the word. Rather, throughout government, in every agency and department, there should be ten percent fewer employees by the year 2001 than exist today. This would apply everywhere except in the legislative and executive (White House employees) branches, where the reduction should be by 20 percent and completed on the same schedule. The same effort should extend to state, county, and city governments.

When determining which programs can be eliminated from government, standards described by Peter F. Drucker in his book, *The New Realities*, should be applied to each program to determine its viability. Those standards are: (1) the program in question must be the only way to achieve an objective; (2) the program must not yet have achieved the objective; (3) the program must not exist to serve political purposes, but rather it must remain narrowly focused on specific performance for the public; and (4) the assumptions upon which the government originally based its decision to implement the program must remain unchanged. Failure to meet any one of these criteria is sufficient to eliminate the program.

Next, redefinition. A valuable process of redefinition is described by Richard Tanner Pascale in his book *Managing on the Edge*. According to Pascale, sick organizations tend to avoid conflict at all costs. They become stagnant and moribund. Efficiency declines, innovation slows, and decay begins. This sounds like an accurate description of our government.

Pascale analyzed Honda Motor Company and identified four critical ingredients used to master conflict within the organization, allowing it to grow, improve, maintain highest standards of quality, and succeed in achieving its mission. Those attributes or elements are, "a deeply ingrained habit of self-questioning, obsessive attention to external(s)..., a drive to do things better than the best in the industry, and a well- tuned system for managing the contention that the previous three factors generate."

Under Pascale's system, the forces for coherence within an organization (represented by shared values and teamwork) struggle against forces of autonomy and self-initiative. The contention between the two leads to innovation and improvements. "By honoring the importance of opposites, we tap into a source of energy that can keep a company alive," says Pascale. His observations proved to him that "contention is an ingredient of organizational life. Our mistake has been to ignore, suppress, or undermanage it." He argues that harnessing contention, turning it into constructive tension, improves organization performance, and leads to "transformation," or the revitalization of the organization.

Never has an organization been more in need of revitalization than the United States government. Other governmental bodies in the United States, ranging from school districts to county, state and local city governments, are close behind in terms of needing revitalization.

Specifically, every department, every office, every agency should apply the principles offered by Pascale to its operation. Devices such as the Administrative Procedures Act, which tend to suppress conflict by turning it into a bureaucratic blizzard of paper, administrative hearings, and "rule making procedures," should be amended or repealed.

The original design of the United States Government achieved a rather effective conflict management. The division of power between the various branches, and the inability of any one branch to dominate, maintained a level of conflict within the country that continually revitalized government. With the exception of the Civil War, the system worked. Passage of the Administrative Procedures Act, however, fixed something that had not broken.

Congress is the arena where the policy conflicts of this

nation are resolved in the open, subjected to the will of the people or their Congressional representatives. The Administrative Procedures Act effectively resolves (suppresses) most conflict at a "staff" level where the process is most susceptible to manipulation by paid professionals employed for that purpose. Congress has reduced itself to a debating society where virtually every Representative and Senator has a committee, sub-committee, or special committee which functions as a media and campaign platform to assure his or her reelection.

In effect, the real business of government is left to the "fourth branch" — those bureaucrats who usually only want to avoid conflict, maintain their positions, and get through each day with a minimum of hassle. Thus, the government is progressively becoming less effective and more stagnant, despite the best efforts of all involved to make it better. The conflict which is now dealt with is often superficial. Who cares about, or will even remember the flap about John Sununu's travel habits? The attempts to come to grips with really critical issues almost inevitably degenerate into the embarrassing moment. For example, recall when the balanced budget resolution was recently scuttled by rank and file members of both parties, in defiance of the President and the Congressional "leadership."

The theory of social contract and government by which we operate advocates a basic separation of powers with strict limits. Locke's view presumes that the legislative function is critically important as a place where policy is set and interests balanced. Constitutionally, the legislature is not permitted to delegate these functions. The Supreme Court has recognized this Constitutional prohibition; what is meant by delegation of legislative power has been finessed, however, to allow for rule making under broadly written legislation, to effectively allow executive branch regulators to legislate.

At the same time, these same regulators can hold administrative hearings before administrative law judges, thus usurping the role of the judicial branch. The net result is an aggregation of real power into one branch of government, the executive, which clearly goes beyond the safeguards established in the United States Constitution. This is allowed to happen in the name of convenience or expediency.

A *Washington Post* article from September 21, 1991, points out the blatant maneuvers of the executive branch to soften the Clean Air Act, against the expressed wishes of Congress. According to the article, when the administration drafted rules to implement the new Clean Air Act, it included a special provision that had been soundly rebuffed by Congress and deleted from the bill finally approved by both House and Senate. The article's author, Michael Weisskopf, said, "The proposed rule is one illustration of how the administration . . . is using the rule-making process to achieve exemptions for industry that were rejected by Congress." This is a prime example of the alteration of Congressional intent by the bureaucracy.

The key is to recapture the policy debate from the Administrative Procedures Act, and thus reposition the conflict about issues to the correct arena: before elected officials and the people. By the same token the judicial branch should be doing the judging. Bureaucrats should spend their time and energy helping citizens to live their lives more easily, maintain their liberty, and successfully pursue happiness. Bureaucrats should not make policy in place of the Legislature, nor should they engage in judicial review in place of the Judiciary.

Congress must stop arguing about trivia and focus on the real issues confronting our nation: money, its value, trade, the deficit, and so on. Congress cannot afford to continue its obsession with the media coverage received from sitting on superfluous committees. The nation witnessed a level of deliberation, leadership, and good faith during the Congressional debate regarding the use of force in the Persian Gulf that should represent the standard of behavior, rather than the exception. To help facilitate this type of focus, the President should be given a line item veto.

Even if we succeed in achieving the reduction and redefinition of government described on these pages, we can and probably will still fail to make government work. In the final analysis government is people - people who act or fail to act in a manner consistent with the basic spirit of the Constitution. Therefore, every elected, appointed, or civil service employee of the government should know, understand, acept, and rededicate himself or herself to the mission statement of the United States of America as set forth in the Preamble of the United States Constitution. This is the law of the land. It should be read, understood, and discussed. Based on such guidelines, every unit of government should define a mission statement consistent with the Preamble and engage in the exercises contained in Chapter Eighteen, "Our Quality of Life."

DECENTRALIZE THE FEDERAL GOVERNMENT.

Employees of the Department of Agriculture would be more effective and less susceptible to "Potomac Fever" if their headquarters were located in Omaha or Kansas City. NASA might as well be in Orlando, or Huntsville, or Houston as Washington, D.C. The headquarters of the Department of Housing and Urban Development could easily be located in Chicago, St. Louis, Denver, or Atlanta. The Federal Communications Commission would be just as effective in New York or Los Angeles.

These are just a few examples to make the point that the government, or at least many of its agencies, could really be a lot closer to the people if relocated away from the insular world "inside the beltway," where the interests of lobbyists too often take precedence over the interests of the taxpaying citizen. Regulators should be forced to look the regulated in the eye at the check-out stand, instead of through the prism of the administrative hearing.

REFORM THE POLITICAL PROCESS.

Most mistakes in government start out as well-intentioned reforms that go wrong. The infamous political action committee (PAC) began as a well-meaning device to make sure all political money stayed above the table and was publicly disclosed. It did what it was designed to do and more, and now reformers bemoan the power of PACs.

Following are seven specific proposals for political reforms which will make it possible to choose leaders who are more responsive to the taxpaying citizen:

1. Expand the matching fund financing arrangement to all federal offices. Matching funds are currently available only for Presidential races.

2. Candidates accepting matching funds for any office should be required to participate in a series of four "no holds barred" debates using the Lincoln/Douglas format. Under this format, candidates debate each other without benefit of a moderator or questioners; this format requires them to think and respond to each other, rather than recite prepared answers from memory. These debates will be carried on radio and television using time purchased by the government. Each

debate should be aired in several time slots to assure easy voter access to information regarding the candidates and their positions.

3. Ease qualification regulations for minor parties.

4. Move election day to Sunday.

5. Create 150 additional Congressional Districts to make the ratio of representatives to citizens more realistic and manageable. This would provide citizens easier access to their representatives, which after all was the purpose of the lower house.

6. Establish universal registration for any person over eighteen in possession of a Social Security card.

7. Establish the right of recall for every federal elected and appointed official within the jurisdiction in which he or she serves.

There are two other potential reforms which it may be appropriate to implement, under certain conditions. The first of these is the concept of "term limitations" for elected officials. First advocated by Thomas Paine, the idea of limiting time in office was defeated by just one vote in the Continental Congress. The call for term limitations today reflects the frustration felt by Americans who, despite the best efforts of elected leaders, are smart enough to see that the recent electoral reform, together with money funneled to incumbents by political action committees, is designed to protect incumbents. Term limitations can be supported only if the following conditions are met:

First, the Administrative Procedures Act (APA) revision discussed previously must be implemented. The current situation in which a professional bureaucracy is able to make policy, "legislate" through rule or regulation writing, and "adjudicate" using administrative hearings, gives the bureaucrat the ability to control the context within which

131

elected officials serve, and thus "sandbag" any initiative not to the liking of the bureaucracy. The only current antidote is the ability of certain politicians to survive long enough to acquire effectiveness by learning how the game is played. How much worse would the Savings and Loan crisis be if there were no "old pro" like Representative Henry B. Gonzalez on the scene to cut through the regulators' bunk? If the APA is revised, term limitations could be allowed.

Second, term limitations could be acceptable if the matching fund approach to financing elections were implemented, and the effect of PACs limited. Under the current process of PAC campaign financing, political action committee operators will become increasingly dominant. Unless we are prepared to see PACs begin to control certain seats, especially in the House of Representatives, and live with the Honorable Representative of Standard Oil or whatever, we should not create term limitations without a financing program to enable candidates without personal wealth or rich backers to compete.

A final word about term limitations — if established, the term limit should not be made too short to allow for adequate on-the-job training. Effectiveness cannot be learned overnight.

The other reform being popularly considered at this moment is the concept of a national process of initiative and referendum. Initiative is the process by which voters can petition for a ballot spot, into which they can insert a policy proposal; referendum involves the referral of a measure by the legislature to a vote of the people.

I am familiar with both the theory and practice of these tools, having made myself a mini-career by consulting to more than a dozen such campaigns. The National Referendum is not a good idea because it basically gives Congress an easy way of avoiding tough issues, by placing politically volatile issues before a general vote. Also, all too often special interest groups petition their friends in the legislature in an effort to confuse an upcoming initiative election: by referring contradictory, confusing, and/or redundant measures to the same ballot, they leave voters wading through muck, trying to sort out who's on first and what's on second. Legislators should legislate, not involve themselves in ballot politics.

Initiatives at the national level would be acceptable if the National Initiative would only appear on the ballot in a national election — special elections should not be scheduled. Also, a matching fund approach for initiative campaigns which operate under strict spending limitations should be available after the measure has qualified for the ballot. No federal funds should be available to finance the gathering of signatures, and the process should not be started without first assuring that the resources will be available for a spirited debate of the measure. Finally, all signatures should be collected within a three and a half year cycle, beginning after the last national election. The number of signatures required should equal one percent of the votes cast for President, signers should be qualified electors at the time of signing, and signatures should be gathered from each state in proportion to the number of votes that state cast in the preceding Presidential election. If all of this is part of the package, the National Initiative would work.

Beyond these reforms, the most basic way to make the American political process work is to change the number of people participating in the arena, and to raise the skill levels of all (even the casual) participants. This will change the nature of the political process. The discussion earlier in this chapter relating to Pascale's theory of revitalization of business organizations through the management of conflict applies just as well to revitalizing the hurley-burley of politics. We need fewer professionals, and more passion.

As an early 20th century thinker named Albert Jay Nock said, "A nation's life consists not in the abundance of things that it possesses; it is the spirit and manners of a people and not the bewildering multiplicity of its social mechanisms that determines the quality of its civilization."

OWN YOUR PROBLEMS, ADMIT YOUR MISTAKES; "JUDGE NOT, THAT YE BE NOT JUDGED."

This is my prayer for peace and civility in our daily lives: we create our own reality and the present is our point of power.

We all tend to blame others for our problems. If we cannot find a person to blame, we find a thing. But, if we go back far enough and look honestly, we can always find a personal decision, statement, failure to act, or belief which directly caused the current trouble, or set us on the path where we find ourselves today. Physical or mental disabilities (except perhaps depression) are the only possible exceptions to this rule that I know of.

Every day each of us chooses what we do. If we are unhappy with the life we are leading, we can choose to change it. It may not be without cost, but we can change our circumstances.

The majority of us seek scapegoats who can be assigned responsibility for what we do not like or cannot accept. All too often we prove our worth to ourselves by putting someone else down. The best known example of this was the Holocaust. Stalin did likewise against landowning peasants shortly after he took power (in fact, he probably killed more people than Hitler), but the all-time champion was probably Mao, who killed tens of millions. All of these victims were scapegoats — dehumanized, then destroyed to hide the heinous iniquity of each leaders' policies.

Anyone disagreeing with the foregoing assessment should visit a bookstore or the library and pick up a book written by Paul Johnson called *Modern Times: The World from the Twenties to the Eighties*. Johnson does an excellent job of describing exactly what happened to entire populations when their leaders chose to resort to scapegoating fear.

Racial, ethnic, or religious minorities are often used to scare people into doing whatever politicians want. We have all heard of Willie Horton, a convicted murderer, whose crime of rape while on furlough from a Massachusetts prison became grist for the mill in George Bush's presidential campaign against Michael Dukakis. We all know about David Duke, who has failed to escape his history with the Ku Klux Klan, although he claims a reversal of heart. Fear has always been a legitimate political tool, and still is. The Governor of Virginia recently evoked fear of Catholics in an effort to attack the nomination of Clarence Thomas to the United States Supreme Court. People concerned about civil liberties and the right to choose had earlier scared the public over another nominee to the Supreme Court, Robert Bork. During the 1940s the United States used fear to justify putting thousands of American citizens into concentration camps because of their race. Taking the western territory from the Native American was justified on the basis of fear, and oppression of African-Americans following the Civil War which continues today relies on fear. Fear is used because it works.

With the passage of time, we have grown more sophisticated. It is no longer acceptable to call someone "Nigger" or "Jap" or "Spik" or "Kike" or "Mick" or "Honkey" or

"Broad". Now, we use code words. "Quota" and "Affirmative Action" are currently in vogue. Nevertheless, we still tell jokes about various groups. It enables us somehow to feel better about ourselves at the expense of others.

The fact is, whatever our race, gender, sexual orientation, or religion, we continue to take advantage of those who are different. If you are a woman, you still earn less than two-thirds of men performing the same job. If you are a Black or Hispanic you earn less, die younger, suffer more violence, and spend more time in jail.

If you are White, you probably feel taken advantage of because you fear that Affirmative Action may prevent you from securing that job you are most qualified for. Or you may feel that it is white, middle-class America who pays all the taxes to support all the social programs to benefit everyone but you. Or you may think the Japanese are taking over America, even though they lag far behind the British and several other nationalities. The bottom line is, it is easier to scapegoat the others because they are "different."

So, we all have someone to fear, if we choose to fear. There is nothing particularly wrong with trying to use fear as a motivating factor in politics. The problem is that we voters allow the use of fear to manipulate our thoughts and actions. We do not take responsibility for our own lives often enough, and we allow ourselves to be victims too frequently. It is time we stopped. Each of us is a human being equipped with hopes and fears, wants and needs. Give your neighbor a chance. Smile at a stranger. Say hello to someone. Say please and thank you. Please, be polite.

ESTABLISH A HOMESTEAD PROGRAM.

The farm crisis, the S & L crisis, and the upcoming bank crisis have caused millions of homes and acres of land to pass to the federal government to be dealt with by the boondoggling Resolution Trust Corporation (RTC), and countless more properties are destined for the same fate. Since too many Americans are homeless and unemployed, and since what the RTC has repossessed cannot be sold for a reasonable price nine times out of ten (and much of what it does sell ends up in foreign hands), why not give it away to American citizens?

Using the model of the "Homestead Act" passed in the last century, why not quickly put this land and these homes back into productive use? Why not help in a meaningful way those Americans who need help?

END ENTITLEMENTS.

The only things Americans should be entitled to are our Constitutional rights. Government can run a retirement or health insurance program, if it wants to, but only if the program is voluntary.

Of course the government must continue to honor its social contract with those who currently participate in Social Security, Medicare, Medicaid, and various government employee retirement programs. However, anyone over the age of fifty or already receiving retirement benefits should be given the option to continue receiving their benefits or receiving a lump sum settlement equal to the total value of their present contributions. Those under fifty would receive a lump sum payment of their contributions in the form of U.S. Savings Bonds, or could continue to participate in Social Security or equivalent programs on a voluntary basis, as they chose. If these programs could sustain themselves in such a way, then good for them. If not, then the government ought to extricate itself from this business.

Second, all retirement programs, whether they be Social Security, federal employee programs, or military retirement programs, should be merged into one combined program with equivalent benefits.

Third, Medicare and Medicaid should be altered to eliminate the waste in the system. Doctors will be encouraged to use their two years of public service (discussed earlier) to provide health care for these program recipients at no charge. The encouragement will probably have to take the form of a franchise tax: in exchange for the educational subsidy attached to medical education, and for being granted a license to practice medicine, the doctor would agree to devote two years of his or her practice to these patients. Hospitals, drug companies, and other suppliers would still receive government compensation at cost for the services provided.

In his book, *The Roaring '80s*, the contemporary Adam Smith (pseudonym for George J.W. Goodman), who hosts the PBS program "Adam Smith's Money World," cites an unidentified director of the Bank of Japan describing Japanese savings habits. He attributed the high rate of Japanese savings at least in part to the lack of an "elaborate social security" system in Japan, which forces the people of Japan to plan ahead and save to "take care of one's parents and to educate one's children." This is a different perspective on the advantages and disadvantages of entitlements here in the United States.

LOOK TO THE FUTURE.

America and the world are posed on the threshold of a New Frontier first defined by John F. Kennedy in the 1960s. The American effort to explore space and take economic advantage of it has been put in the hands of a bureaucracy known as the National Aeronautics and Space Administration (NASA). NASA did a great job of putting U.S. astronauts on the moon before the Russians could get there. NASA has not done such a great job of making space economically useful, however, even though it is generally agreed that there exists an incredible potential for economic development in space.

A Princeton University professor, Gerard O'Neill, proposed establishing space cities constructed of material mined from the moon. He would position these cities in an orbit between the earth and the moon at a level where the gravitational influences of the earth, the moon, and the sun equalize or cancel each other out. When positioned at one of these "Legrange points," a city can theoretically remain in place forever. O'Neill predicts that cities with as many as 10,000 inhabitants could be constructed at these points, and made economically viable by, for example, using solar energy to generate electricity. This electricity could then be transmitted to earth or used to make those products best manufactured in a vacuum or weightless state. Even if O'Neill's ideas are not proven correct over the next few hundred years, space has shown that there is great potential for economic development. Every day each of us benefits from communication satellites, weather satellites, and materials with wide-spread commercial utility (teflon, for example) that were originally developed for the space program.

The problem is that NASA, being a bureaucracy, is focused on bureaucratic needs, as opposed to economic needs. Because NASA is so concerned about maintaining its prerogatives and position within the organization of the federal government, fighting for appropriations and maintaining perks, the U.S. space program is missing opportunities. Some payloads have to wait as long as eight years to get into orbit; others, after they get into orbit, do not work. The Hubble space telescope is a good example of both of these trends. Yet, NASA claims that it has adequate lift capacity to get the job done.

Ben Bova and Stephen L. Gillett, writing in *Omni* magazine, offered two possible solutions designed to bring private capital to bear on the exploration of space, so that space can pay for itself rather than costing the taxpayers billions of dollars. Their first model for opening up the "New Frontier" is based on the Pacific Railroad Act of 1862, which was passed to finance the construction of a transcontinental railroad. "The Act set up a system of federal loans, repayable over thirty years, to fund the expansion," they wrote. "It also granted land from the public domain along the right-of-way. By 1871, more than 130 million additional acres had been given to the railroads. This was a painless subsidy, which did not involve spending taxpayers' money."

Their second model is inspired by the Phoenix-area Salt River Project (SRP), which was launched after the Reclamation Service (now called the Bureau of Reclamation) was established. The Salt River Project was designed in 1903 to provide irrigation water for farmers. Because the project also generated electricity as a by-product, the project sold the electricity to the city of Phoenix, essentially subsidizing the delivery of irrigation water. By 1917, the project was turned over to the landowners who used its water; it is managed by an elected board of directors to this day. Federal funds used to construct the SRP's system of dams, canals, generating stations, and power lines have long since been repaid. The SRP's Roosevelt Dam was the first of its kind to generate electricity.

These two examples show how government and private

industry have, and could, work together to create entirely new industries. This seems the most productive approach toward exploration of the "New Frontier." These techniques can also be used to enable state and local government to rebuild decayed infrastructure, private sector organizations to raise needed capital resources to explore new technologies on earth (High Definition Television and "Maglev" trains, for example), and existing institutions to adapt to a changing world (such as education). Although debt would be incurred, it is debt to improve productivity and competitiveness rather than debt to facilitate instant gratification through consumer consumption, thus it is justified.

Chapter Fourteen

Change The World IV:
Environment & Homes: On a Human Scale

WITH REGARD FOR OUR ENVIRONMENT WE MUST
PRACTICE WHAT WE PREACH.

Most of us have lived through two "Earth Days," and
more of us every day are trying not to inflict any more pain
on the earth and helping to repair the damage done to it.
Billions of dollars are now being spent to protect the
environment, and millions more are spent telling us which
products are environmentally safe and what our good corporate citizens are doing to protect the environment, or
clean up yesterday's messes. Despite the fervor, Califor-
nians recently voted down the most comprehensive environmental initiative, called "Big Blue," ever put before voters.
What is really happening?

Is the Chesapeake Bay recovering or dying? Can the
Everglades be saved? Will the Brazilians stop slash and
burn land clearing before they destroy the Amazon Rain
Forest? Can Eastern Europe be detoxified? What environmental price is being paid in Asia for all of the industrial
development there in the last thirty years? Do we or will we
have enough fresh water to drink? Are pesticides destroying
life in the soil and leading to so much soil erosion that we
are in danger of running out of food? Is the hole in the
ozone getting worse? Is the globe really warming? What

will we do with the garbage? Which is worse, acid rain or nuclear waste?

There may be no single good solution right now to protect our environment, although I can guarantee there will be more legislation. It will probably be years before we truly understand the environment, if we ever do.

So, starting here and now, where do we go? A friend of mine in a high school debate about tobacco once said, "I'm not going to stop smoking. By the time I get lung cancer a cure will have been discovered." That attitude summarizes one possible approach to our environmental problems. The opposite is to assume a point of view based on civil disobedience — the "ecoterrorism" approach to force change as advocated by Earth First. Both alternatives should be rejected.

There is a third possibility. Each and every one of us can begin to lead a life in balance with our environment. Every day, in everything we do, we can act in a manner more in harmony with nature than the way we acted the day before. We can live the solution to our problems by adopting an ethic of environmental awareness and concern, basing our actions on principles of good stewardship of the earth, leaving it at least a little better and certainly no worse than we found it.

The best description of such a philosophy was written in the 1850s by an Indian Chief named Seattle, in response to an offer by the U. S. Government to buy his tribe's land. Here are some excerpts:

> The President in Washington sends word that he
> wishes to buy our land. But how can you buy or sell
> the sky? The land? The idea is strange to us. If we do
> not own the freshness of the air and the sparkle of the
> water, how can you buy them? . . .

We know the sap which courses through the trees as we know the blood that courses through our veins. We are part of the earth, and it is part of us. The perfumed flowers are our sisters. The bear, the deer, the great eagle, these are our brothers. The rocky crests, the juices in the meadow, the body heat of the pony, and the man, all belong to the same family. . . .

If we sell you the land, remember that the air is precious to us, that the air shares its spirit with all the life it supports. The wind that gave our grandfather his first breath also receives his last sigh. The wind also gives our children the spirit of life. So if we sell you our land, you must keep it apart and sacred, as a place where a man can go to taste the wind that is sweetened by the meadow flowers.

Will you teach your children what we have taught our children? That the earth is our mother? What befalls the earth befalls all the sons of the earth.

This we know, the earth does not belong to man, man belongs to the earth. All things are connected like the blood that unites us all. Man did not weave the web of life, he is merely a strand in it. Whatever he does to the web, he does to himself. . . .

Your destiny is a mystery to us. What will happen when the buffalo are all slaughtered? The wild horses tamed? What will happen when the secret corners of the forest are heavy with the scent of many men and the view of the ripe hills is blotted by the talking wires? Where will the thicket be? GONE! And what

is it to say goodbye to the swift pony and the hunt?
The end of living and the beginning of survival.

Chief Seattle says it better than most environmental
activists. His advice is valuable, regardless of the facts,
theories, and techniques that we will eventually discover to
answer the questions which began this section.

We should not need to pass any more laws — we have
plenty of laws. By now everyone knows what is at stake.
What we need to do is practice what we preach. We should
all be separating our garbage, and participating in recycling.
We should all be sharing the ride, or using mass transit, or
riding bicycles. We should all be conscious of our business
decisions and their impact on the environment. We should
all know what impact we have when we adjust our thermo-
stats, light our barbecues, or wash the laundry. We should
all know what it means when we flush the toilet, or leave the
water running while brushing our teeth. We should know
where a candidate is likely to lead us if elected, and the
impact of public policies which we can affect. We should
know about the companies we invest in, and their relationship with Mother Earth. And we should teach our children
these things.

The earth will adjust and maintain a balance regardless
of what we do, and life will be encouraged in some fashion.
If the balance is altered because we dump too much phos-
phate and nitrogen into the Chesapeake Bay, nature will
react to create a vast algae bloom to consume the excess
chemicals. Unfortunately, algae displaces other organisms
such as rockfish, clams, oysters, and crab, but from nature's
point of view, a balance is maintained.

Nature will always maintain a balance. Take away the
ozone and pay the price in skin cancer and increased species

mutation. Close one niche with acid rain, and another will inevitably be created. The danger is more than choosing between a crab and algae. The danger is in Chief Seattle's warning: "The end of living and the beginning of survival." Are we willing to risk changing our lifestyle in order to live, or will we keep on until we are forced to merely survive?

The choice is ours, as is the responsibility. It is time we practice what we preach every moment of every day in every way.

OUR HOMES AND OUR TOWNS MUST BECOME HUMAN SCALE.

During the middle of the 1970s a movement began to prevent the "Californication of Arizona." Some folks were motivated to join the movement by sincere environmental concern, while others were more selfishly motivated, trying to protect the "nicer" areas from low-income or high-density development. All instinctively recognized that what had happened in California was not quite right, but no one could really articulate what was wrong. What went on in Arizona was not unique. In almost infinite variations, the same issues have been raised and the same battles fought throughout America.

Recent articles in *Smithsonian* and *Time* magazines reported both a definition of the problem of what we used to call "Californication" and articulated a solution for it. The articles described the work of Andres Duany and Elizabeth Plater-Zyberk, a husband/wife team of architects and town planners dedicated to restoring suburban development to human scale and making it possible to build mixed use communities that are profitable, yet accessible to a wide range of income groups.

The *Smithsonian* article profiled a town called Seaside,

Florida, calling it a "planned community designedly striving to combine the best of what used to be with life today, in keeping an eye to the future." The 80 acre town, now over a decade in the making, will eventually have about 300 homes. No house is more than a 15 minute walk from any other. The streets are narrow and the plan features a consistent design style. The community has been deemed a great success.

Time magazine describes "the building blocks" of these "Oldfangled New Towns" as:

1. Town centers which create a commercial downtown within walking distance of any home;

2. Huddled houses built close together to encourage the sense of community;

3. Streets which are narrow and well designed for pedestrians;

4. Architectural style and scale which is both consistent and engaging; and

5. Civic landmarks featuring public buildings and park settings to function as focal points.

According to Elizabeth Plater-Zyberk, after World War II a bias by Veterans' Administration loan officers toward new construction sent people to the suburbs, decanting urban neighborhoods and downtown commercial centers. Abundant federal dollars went to road construction, while public transportation was largely ignored. Modern land use planning divided social and income groups even more.

To overcome auto-dependent suburban sprawl, Zyberk and Duany advocate the creation of new towns similar to Seaside, Florida, made up of complete neighborhoods containing town centers and greenbelts. In existing cities, they suggest incentives such as tax credits for single vehicle ownership, home-ownership in the city core, the relocation of businesses and industry to the city, and the addition of subsidiary rental units to existing single-family homes as a means to encourage rebuilding of city centers. They also believe the auto industry should be required to spend as much on public transit and research into alternative vehicles as they do on advertising their automobiles.

Their last recommendation is probably ill-advised, given the current debility of our auto industry, but their approach to, quoting Zyberk, "restructure the city for the redistribution of resources" makes sense.

Elizabeth Plater-Zyberk and Andres Duany have designed a model building and planning code which can be introduced to your local government, if this is an area of concern for you. Contact them for more information at 1023 Southwest 25th Avenue, Miami, Florida 33135.

Chapter Fifteen

Change The World V:
Foreign Policy and Defense: America First

ADDRESSING THE ISSUE of foreign policy, syndicated columnist, turned presidential candidate, Patrick J. Buchanan recently wrote, "The incivility and brutality of our cities, the fading away of the Reagan Boom, the rise of ethnic hatred, are concentrating the minds of Americans on their own society. What doth it profit a nation if it gain the whole world, and lose its own soul?" He offered seven specific foreign policy recommendations which will help put "America First," as he calls it.

1. Dissolve the Rio Treaty and return to a narrower version of the Monroe Doctrine; putting this another way, leave South America to the South Americans;

2. Withdraw American troops from Korea;

3. Abrogate, or repeal, the mutual security treaty with Japan;

4. Reject extension of the North Atlantic Treaty Organization (NATO) into Eastern Europe;

5. As Soviet troops withdraw from Eastern Europe and Germany, match that withdrawal with an American departure from Europe, culminating with the American withdrawal from NATO;

6. End foreign aid, shut down the Agency for International Development, and scale down the United States

Information Agency while the United States withdraws from the African, Asian, and Latin American Development Banks. Resources saved should be devoted to domestic development; and

7. Stop Congress from giving money to the International Monetary Fund or the World Bank because, Buchanan says, "both are global S&Ls; and we are going to have to pay off the lion's share of the lousy paper."

Buchanan's ideas have at least some merit and are worthy of careful consideration. However, it is not appropriate to just walk away from the rest of the world. Isolationism is no longer a viable alternative. Rather, if Buchanan's suggestions are implemented, America must fill the vacuum which results by undertaking a series of alternative actions.

These actions should be aimed toward creating a process to replace U.S. government presence in foreign lands with a U.S. business presence. This could be supported by a venture capital fund to facilitate development of world markets by U.S. companies; it could be administered by an industry/government partnership structured on the model of the Federal Reserve and funded with a one-time capital investment equal to one year's foreign aid expenditures of 15 billion dollars.

Whatever our government finally decides, it is clear that a foreign policy based on a New World Order with the United States playing the role of global cop is dangerous in a world where nationalistic and ethnic tensions are the new reality. American troops need not be risked to maintain order in Serbia, Croatia, Moldavia, or any other place where Americans and American interests are not at issue. In the case of Iraq, it is difficult to understand why we deployed troops to the Persian Gulf. If we sought to protect the interests of Israel or Kuwait, we should not have become involved — it is not our responsibility to protect someone else's national interest. If we sought to protect the interests of Western Europe and Japan, who depend on oil from Iraq and Kuwait, then American troops should not have been endangered to assure continued access to cheap energy. Such cheap energy merely subsidizes the ability of Japan and Western Europe to compete with American economic interests. If the purpose was to stop another Hitler who was about to become a nuclear power and to avert a preemptive nuclear strike by Israel, then the right action was taken. From what has been disclosed, we may never know which of these reasons led to our drawing the line in the sand, although I believe there was a real nuclear threat which justified the actions taken. Whatever the reason, the situation illustrates the dangers associated with maintaining a New World Order, a.k.a. Pax Americana, by force of arms. Risks are huge and decisions cannot be made in the heat of emotion.

The new reality in today's foreign policy was perhaps first recognized by Peter Drucker. He pointed out that the anticipated (at the time he wrote) demise of the Soviet empire would usher in an era of increasing danger as the period of enforced peace guaranteed by the doctrine of "Mutual Assured Destruction" ended. The dangers of nuclear weapons falling into the hands of unstable leaders or small nations at war with one another cannot be underestimated. Nor is the lack of a delivery system a deterrent, since, as Drucker points out, a terrorist could simply mail a nuclear weapon to a Manhattan address where its detonation would have disastrous effect. Any country's foreign policy today must be conducted with awareness and appreciation of the interdependency of all countries on one another. The era of confrontation and conflict of arms is rapidly becoming (if it is not already) obsolete. The key is now cooperation.

What does this foreign policy of cooperation mean to the future of the defense establishment? About three million Americans (not counting defense industry employees) are engaged in the defense of our country. In the era of Adam Smith, these people were not considered productive members of society. However, in *The New Realities*, Peter Drucker points out that for a period of a couple of hundred years culminating in World War II, "The defense economy and the civilian peacetime economy moved in tandem, mutually enriching each other." Drucker cites the invention of the cargo ship, steam engine, computer, modern transportation systems, and biotechnology as examples of military developments which significantly improved civilian life. Conversely, the automobile, airplane, telephone, and radio are examples of civilian developments which dramatically enhanced military capability.

"But now this is over," Drucker wrote. "Indeed, we now know that defense spending and defense technology are serious drains on the civilian economy. That the Japanese spend very little money on defense and even less on defense research and technology is, as everyone now admits, a major strength. In contrast, the heavy defense burden in the United States is a major — perhaps the major — cause of the loss of competitive strength and leadership of the American ecomony. The even larger portion of gross national product that goes into defense in Russia is surely one of the major causes for the backwardness and continuing deterioration of the Russian economy."

According to Drucker, the problem is not money, but people. He explained that Japanese scientists work for the civilian economy rather than in defense. In comparison, as many as one-third of American engineers are employed in defense, and in Russia, virtually all competent scientists and technologists have been employed in defense work. This concentration on defense rather than consumer production is disastrous to an economy.

Drucker makes the point that "defense is no longer possible; only retaliation is. Arms are no longer an effective tool of policy." However, it is hardly possible or prudent to force hasty and draconian cuts on the military in this era of heightened tensions. The course being followed by the United States government which calls for a rethinking of American military doctrine in light of changing conditions, de-emphasis of costly new weapons systems designed to fight a European war against the Soviet Union, and a gradual 25 percent reduction of force levels is correct. It is in the best interest of all Americans to transfer the talent, "can-do" attitude, and resources made available by this "peace dividend" to the new economic and technological battlefields as quickly as possible. Whatever decisions are made, it is important that all Americans heed the advice of President Theodore Roosevelt to "speak softly and carry a big stick."

Chapter Sixteen

Holistic Politics

THE RECOMMENDATIONS MADE in the previous seven chapters are not independent of one another. Sound money; fair trade; tax reform; universal public service; rational drug policy; revitalization of government; decentralization of government; environmental, educational, and health programs that work; and accepting our own responsibility to make the system succeed, rather than reacting fearfully to manipulation, constitute a common sense holistic approach to Reinventing America. Partial solutions will fail. Waiting for someone else to clean up the mess for us will fail.

Everything I suggest may well be wrong. But before accepting substitutes, check to see that they are comprehensive in scope and deal with the underlying causes of our problems as well as the symptoms. Any program which fails to address the economic foundations of this country will merely, in the words of Walter Reuther, President of the United Autoworkers in the '40s, "... negotiate the wooden nickels of inflation."

Whether you agree or disagree with me about these issues, do not abdicate your responsibility to take control of your life and the life of your country. In 1961, John F. Kennedy said, "Ask not what your country can do for you. Ask what you can do for your country." Today, thirty years later, the country is in deep trouble and his sentiment is not as fashionable. Today, the best thing we can do for our country is to forsake our seats in the grandstand and get down on the field. We cannot afford the luxury of being bystanders any longer. Our country, our lifestyle, our jobs, and our future are at risk. We should seize the moment and act now to protect our interests.

Sharing these ideas about the problems damaging the machinery of American government may well cause some readers to get lost in the process of becoming mechanics. The material in this section of *Reinventing America* is not intended to serve as the nucleus of a reform movement. This is not intended as material for a political campaign, a recommended party platform, or a legislative program. My hope for our government and society is that a sufficient number of us will be motivated to dedicate ourselves to living each minute of our lives in a manner consistent with our ideals. In this vein, the preceding chapters are offered as catalysts for thought.

As another catalyst for thought, consider the following. In his book, *The New Realities*, Peter F. Drucker talks about the limits of government. He points out that the question is always couched in terms of what government SHOULD do rather than what government CAN do. As government more frequently fails to perform as promised, more and more people are raising the issues of what functions are appropriate to government, how much should government attempt to do, and what are the limits of government. One critical area of government activism is the economic arena. Drucker correctly points out that the main point of Adam Smith in *The Wealth of Nations* is that "government, by its very nature, cannot run the economy, not even poorly." Smith did not argue that the government should not run the economy, but rather that it cannot. Drucker also cites F.A. Hayek's book, *The Fatal Conceit: The Errors of Socialism*, stating that Hayek "came to the conclusion that the nature of information makes it impossible both in theory and in practice, for government to manage or even to control the economy."

The field of economic management is not the sole area in which governments fail to perform. Drucker cites the example of collective farming in the Soviet Union, the "War on Poverty" in the United States, and the Japanese national railroad. He points out that activities undertaken by government become "moral" rather than "economic," saying "it is in the nature of government activities that they come to be seen as symbols and sacred rather than as utilities and means to an end." The inevitable result of this moral/economic dichotomy is that "moral" government programs are not subjected to a rational cost/benefit analysis, and any attempt to trim these programs or activities, regardless of the relative merit of the program, are inevitably attacked as a "sell out" or an "abandonment of principle." As previously discussed, Drucker suggests that an excellent example of this problem is the history of efforts to eradicate drug abuse in the United States. He comes to the difficult conclusion that the only solution might be to attack the problem economically by removing the profit motive.

When can government functions prove successful? As previously mentioned, Drucker identifies several prerequisites for government activities to succeed. Government activity must "remain the only way to do a certain task; that it not outlive its usefulness and not be continued once it has attained its objective; that it not be made to serve political ends, however laudable, but remain narrowly focused on specific performance for the public; and finally that the assumptions on which it is based remain unchanged." If this test is fairly applied to the various functions of government as practiced in these United States, many if not most of those functions will quickly emerge as candidates for termination or privatization.

Governmental power can, in Drucker's view, be effectively used to provide for the common defense, as well as maintain law and order and a system of justice. In addition, Drucker says "government can set ground rules that are equally binding on everybody." These rules assure a "level playing field."

When government abuses its power, as in the case of the Soviet Union, or Hitler's Germany, the nation suffers and can even cease to exist. When government abuses its power to tax, Drucker points out that the economic vitality of a society can be severely damaged. Where the abuse is especially severe, people will merely stop working since they have nothing left to gain if all of the additional income they earn goes into the tax system. Drucker says, "in all countries in which the tax take approaches or exceeds 30 percent of gross personal income, a 'gray economy' develops." There was almost no tax cheating in the United States before 1960. Now, however, we have developed our own gray economy: the federal tax burden exceeds 19 percent of gross personal income, and other taxing authorities increase the total burden to about 35 percent of our paychecks. "How big the gray economy in the United States has now become we do not know — there are of course no figures on it — but estimates range as high as 15 percent of the official economy," Drucker says. In comparison, he points out that the gray economy in Sweden is about 30 percent and in the People's Republic of China it is between one-third to one-half of the total economy.

Power is the reality, but when power is abused, eventually the entire system breaks down and everyone in it suffers. The reality today is that too few of us exercise our power and as a consequence government and the major institutions of society (businesses, financial institutions, health care institutions, labor groups, professional associations, and education institutions) simply go along to get along, doing their job as they see it without consideration for the health and well-being of the whole system, and without thought of the common good. Power is abused, all of us suffer, and no one can really understand why. Each of us can tell a horror story about an encounter with a large, impersonal organization. Each of us intuitively understands that the system is out of control and beginning to resemble a semi-truck roaring downhill with failing brakes. It is up to each of us to accept the responsibility to do something to stop the truck before we totally lose control.

PART FOUR

REINVENTING AMERICA

Ask, and it will be given you; seek and you will find;
knock, and it will be opened to you. For everyone who
asks receives, and he who seeks finds, and to him who
knocks it will be opened.

Matthew, 7:7-8

Chapter Seventeen

Charity Begins at Home

THIS PART OF THE BOOK is designed to provide the skills and techniques necessary to begin changing our world. It is the "nuts and bolts" section, with political advice, techniques, and a methodology to plot the winning strategy. We can apply these skills to any situation which confronts us in our daily life.

We have allowed the decision-makers of our country to be inordinately influenced by the people who will directly benefit from their decisions, rather than looking at the whole picture. That is why, in just one instance, over 100 million dollars is spent annually on lobbyists, lawyers, and public relations professionals representing Japan, who make sure that the interests of their well-funded client are supported by Congress and the Executive Branch. These chapters will give you the opportunity to create a mechanism by which your interests can get equal time, without costing you millions of dollars.

Dozens of books about politics provide policy solutions to correct government's mistakes — they are long on ideas but short on practical information about how to convert those ideas into reality. This section of *Reinventing America* will give concrete suggestions for what we can do today and every day to make a real difference. You will be introduced to techniques to make things happen in your life and the political life of your community, state, and nation.

This will not make any one an expert, nor will it necessarily make a person adept at any of the techniques; however, you will come away knowing where to start to make positive changes in your world. Like anything else in life, by exercising our rights, we can all become more capable.

No one can lead us to some utopian vision of America. Even if someone could, to paraphrase Eugene Debs, a candidate for President around 1912, once we arrived at that utopia someone else could lead us right back to where we started. The answer is to create our own utopian vision and to live it, minute by minute.

The first step is to PAY ATTENTION. What do we do with our time? How much do we earn and how do we spend our money? Are we satisfied with that? If not, why not?

What are we thinking minute to minute, and why? Who is pulling our chain or pushing our buttons? How did they do it? Did the Willie Horton story anger you? How did you feel about the Willie Horton campaign commercial? Why? Does it even matter who or what Willie Horton is?

Every minute of every day we are all thinking thoughts — conducting silent internal dialogues with ourselves. Take a minute and listen to your mind. Most of the time our dialogue is reactive — responding to something we hear, see, or think. Most of the time it is out of control. Just for a minute, turn it off. Close your eyes and empty your head of all the dialogue. It is not easy is it?

Now, follow your thoughts as long as you can. See what direction they take. Most people cannot follow the path of their thoughts for more than a few minutes at a time.

The next time you react to a news story, a television

commercial, a direct mail fundraising letter, a politician's speech, or a sermon, tune in to your reaction. Ask yourself, why did I react that way? Is that what was intended? Who intended that I react that way? And why? Do I really agree with that position (speech, commercial, article, letter)?

The first step to controlling our world is for each of us to take control of our own minds and pay attention to ourselves. Then, we can evaluate our opinions and actions in light of our enlightened self-interest. But how do you we each define our enlightened self-interest?

Think about enlightened self-interest in the context of the current problems with drug use in America. Sure we all feel terrible about drugs. More than that, we are scared to death about the drugs our children may be taking right now. So what is in our self-interest? (Pay attention to the flow of your thoughts as you read the next few paragraphs.)

First, how do we define drugs?

Cocaine, marijuana, and heroin are usually defined as problem drugs. On an occasional basis alcohol is included. But, what about coffee, cocoa, or nicotine? Are problem drugs only those drugs we do not personally use? What makes a drug a problem anyway? How many cases of lung cancer are required before nicotine is added to the dangerous drug list?

I believe that the ultimate political definition of dangerous drugs could be: a drug without a crew of lobbyists, political action committees, a PR program, or an advertising campaign. Therefore, we can forget coffee, tea, nicotine, and alcohol and focus on heroin, cocaine, LSD, crack, PCP, and marijuana.

The political system has taken the task upon itself to define your enlightened self-interest as a variety of things, in a variety of ways:

> "Just say no!"
> *"This is your brain . . . This is your brain on*
> *drugs . . . Any questions?"*
> THE WAR ON DRUGS.
> "DRUGS ARE THE CANCER THAT WILL DESTROY
> AMERICA FROM WITHIN."
> **"Support your local police."**

None of these statements or slogans are very informative, but they conjure up visions that scare the hell out of me. How do you react?

Now, going back to the issue, what are we going to do about drugs?

How about locking up the pushers? Maybe we should bomb the Colombians back into the stone age. Will that solve our problem with our kids? Most people say, just get the pushers out of the schools. So for the sake of discussion, assume that we will lock the pushers up and bomb the source.

What will that do to our taxes? How will it affect the kinds of towns in which we live? What if our children are the ones to get busted? Will it solve the problem?

How many of us have ever considered just talking to our sons or daughters, getting to know them, teaching them about drugs, and listening to their opinions? Pay special attention to how your mind reacted to that thought.

The most effective anti-drug policy might just be playing catch with the kids in the back yard, or spending time with them at a museum talking about art instead of watching television. As corny as it sounds, we need to take some time and get to know our children.

Having thought about that, is it still a good idea to just lock up the pushers and bomb the Colombians? It is often easy to endorse the quick solution. Unfortunately, quick solutions are not always quick and are seldom easy, not to mention cheap. Someone has to pay for the jails and the bombs. Guess who?

I once worked on a project with a man who responded to my objections about costs by saying, "You can pick any two of the following three: good, fast, cheap." Notice that easy was not an option. This rule applies to politics and government as well as commercial endeavors.

For years our "leaders" have given us the quick fix — the easy way out — and where has it put us? In a hell of a mess, that's where. Quick fixes usually do not work.

Back to the subject of drugs, we have decided to get tough. We have locked them up. We have taken the pushers and the users off the street. It sounds good, but think about it for a minute.

We currently imprison more people on a per capita basis than the Soviets or the South Africans. We spend an incredible amount on our police and our prisons. Yet our schools, cities, and children are still a mess, thanks to drugs.

The mess has spread into our courts. If you were to be injured in a car wreck and needed to sue to recover for your damages, you would experience frustrating court delays because criminal cases take priority over your civil suit.

The mess has also spread to all other segments of the economy. Billions of dollars of income are not taxed because those dollars are generated under the table and never appear on a tax form. Bankers have been corrupted to launder money. An immense cash economy outside of the normal system now affects each of us. Call your local librarian for an estimate of the dollars involved annually in the illegal drug trade, then take out your IRS form 1040 and

Charity Begins at Home

figure out how much in taxes the government (i.e., you) have been cheated out of.

Now that we have locked up thousands of people and we still suffer the drug problem, the new and improved answer is to "declare war on the drug kingpins" and call for the death penalty for dealers and pushers. We invade Panama and chase the "extraditables," but nothing much happens. Why? Because there is enough profit in the trade to make the risks worthwhile. Because the law of supply and demand works like a charm.

Do not take my word for any of this. Just for fun, call up a local politician and ask how many new jail cells your state has built in the last ten years, and how many inmates are in jail now as opposed to ten years ago. You might also ask about state population numbers and compute for yourself whether the percentage increase for incarcerations mirrors the percentage increase for population.

Now think about how much those jail cells cost. Would you believe it is more expensive to incarcerate someone for a year than it is to send that person to Harvard for a year? Still, our neighborhoods are not safe.

Try this one on for size: the most likely cause of death for our teenaged sons in America today is gunshot wounds (this statistic is not just referring to young Black men, but to all young men). This is one more hidden cost of the illicit drug trade.

We could go on and on and on about the drug problem in America, but that is not the point of this discussion. I digressed to the issue of drugs because it is an emotional one for most of us. Consequently, we easily fall prey to slick politicians who sell a quick fix in order to get elected, without putting much thought to really solving the problem. Why do we allow this to happen? By now you should know

166

the answer — it is because we usually do not pay attention. We allow our emotions to govern our reactions.

Maybe the quick fix is not to vote for tough lawmakers, appoint tough judges, invade Panama, bomb Columbia, and impose the death sentence on our children who happen to sell drugs. Maybe the quick fix is to spend more time with our children, rather than with our children and the television. And maybe not.

The point is to THINK, not just blindly react to emotional phrases and empty promises. In all phases of our life it is important to PAY ATTENTION!

We tend to live life in a fog of minute-by-minute mental dialogue, blindly reacting to catch phrases that have been cleverly concocted to force us to respond based on instinct or emotion. We are programmed to react according to what is in the politician's (retailer's, manufacturer's, marketer's, or preacher's) enlightened self-interest, rather than our own.

A friend of mine who served in the United States House of Representatives complained that political life required him to spend too much time, effort, and money on "posturing and strutting." He said that voters paid little attention to the substance of his positions, but instead focused on the illusion of slogans.

Think about how much of life is spent on automatic pilot. Have you ever driven someplace and not been able to remember the trip after you arrived? How often do we turn off our children (or our spouse, boss, or co-workers) as they talk to us? How many elections have we skipped? Even worse, how many times have we voted for or against a candidate or an issue because of a party label or because of some advertisement that convincingly told us it was the right thing to do?

We are worried about family, house, friends, job, money,

city, state, country, taxes, and the planet about a tenth of the time. The rest of the time we are in a fog. We are living our lives on automatic pilot. We are not PAYING ATTENTION.

If we want things to improve, we have to take responsibility to make them better. Do not wait for George Bush to do it, he is waiting for you. Spend a couple of hours with C-SPAN to see what I mean. Our elected and appointed officials are just like the rest of us, no better and no worse. If we want the economy to get better and think the government should balance the budget (as most of us do), how can we expect that to happen if we use a charge card for Christmas or birthdays or dinner tonight? Sound economics begins at home.

If we were to balance our budgets, save ten percent of disposable income (which is about half the amount the average Japanese household saves), and lead a productive life by living up to our potential at home, work, or school, it might not seem like much. But, if your household and my household are joined by 100,000 other households in the United States, the impact becomes significant.

That impact is not limited to just dollars and cents, the psyche of the country will have changed. Eventually the folks we elect will get the message. The first step toward implementing a balanced economy is to personally stop living on debt. It is easy to point fingers at City Hall or Washington and blame them for our problems. It is lots tougher to pay cash for goods and services that we really need, and forego instant gratification.

Again, the point is not to talk about balancing our personal economic situation, the point is to become aware that what we do makes a difference. Everything we do makes a difference: voting, spending, borrowing, cutting corners at work, telling little white lies, and not separating the garbage to recycle cans and paper. Each of us creates the world in which we live. If we do not like it, the place to start fixing it is in our own minds. We are what we think. We can hardly expect to fix what is wrong with the world if we cannot straighten out our own lives.

It is said that "charity begins at home," and so does everything else. If we want to balance our country's economy we should start by balancing our home economy. If we want to deal with drugs in America, we need to deal with drugs at home first. If we believe in "law and order," we must live it. A concise expression of this concept has become a popular bumper sticker: Think Globally, Act Locally.

Learning to pay attention will launch us on a journey of discovery. Life will change — not all at once and, in the beginning, not noticeably, but it will change.

Gradually, the process of change will accelerate. We will think more and do more, become more aware, and feel more intensely. We will begin to examine our beliefs and value system, we will begin to question assumptions and make more informed decisions. Close associates may begin to think of us as a pain in the rear end, but their reaction to our honesty is their problem. We should cherish our awakening.

What do you believe about yourself? Most of us do not reflect on ourselves as much as we should. Most of us maintain a series of core beliefs about ourselves which we cannot even articulate. All too many of these core beliefs are negative, and in turn stimulate negative emotions. The beliefs team up with the emotions, resulting in an unhappy and dissatisfying life experience.

Take a moment to write down what you believe about yourself. Are you basically a good person? Are you loyal? Are you successful? Are you honest? Are you capable? Do not stop with these attributes, try to go on for as long as you can.

If there are areas of your life with which you are unhappy, what beliefs do you hold to account for this unhappiness? Write down those beliefs on your list as well.

As you pay attention to your thoughts and emotions, you will find some that arise from beliefs which you missed on the first go-around. Add these beliefs to your list.

After a day or so of this, review your lists. There are probably some items on the list that will surprise and dismay you. As an example, suppose that when you were a child one of your parents implanted in you the belief that you were unworthy for some reason — perhaps you were overweight. Now, years later you feel anxiety about your weight. No matter how much effort you expend to control your weight, how many diets you try, or even what you actually weigh, you feel you are not able to control your weight.

Because of your parent's criticism about your weight, you believe you are overweight. Therefore you are, at least in your own mind. Because of your excess weight, you also believe you are unable to attract a suitable spouse. Therefore you can't. Because you are not married, you believe you must be unhappy. Therefore you are unhappy. It is an unending cycle.

You can invest as much effort in this type of analysis as you care, or dare, to. The more you engage in such analysis the better your understanding will become of the beliefs and emotions which underlie your reality.

The point to grasp is that by understanding them, we all can better control our beliefs. Once a belief is recognized (and that is often the hardest part), it can be accepted, rejected, or amended, and you can begin to take control of your life.

We each create our own reality. Moment by moment

our belief system controls our actions, perceptions, emotions, and opinions. In turn these factors all contribute to the reality we each experience. If your reality is not to your liking, you can change it. When? Right here and now. How? By changing your beliefs, and all that follows will be changed. This is a domino effect — take advantage of it.

"You create your own reality and the present is your point of power," writes Jane Roberts in *The Nature of Personal Reality: A Seth Book*. The implication is that nothing can be done in the past or future. We exist now, in the present; therefore we can exert the maximum leverage to change our reality right now — not yesterday, not next week. Change a belief now, and reality will soon follow. But, how do we change a belief?

Do not deny an unwanted belief — that will only serve to reinforce it. Instead, move beyond the belief. Be positive, not negative. Start by focusing on the belief you want, rather than the existing one. During your quiet times give yourself permission to focus on the new belief. Actually say to yourself:

"I am now going to build a new belief. I recognize that this new belief may not be consistent with all of my existing beliefs, but that's OK. I affirm my personal responsibility to choose my beliefs. I know that I create my own reality and that I live in the present. The present is my point of power."

Next, visualize those past experiences which are consistent with the new belief. Relive happy occasions and review the emotions associated with them; know that now these feelings and emotions are caused by the new belief.

Finally, daydream about what result you will experience once the new belief takes hold. Enjoy yourself. Have fun.

The whole process should take no more than ten to

fifteen minutes each day, then you can relax and forget about it. Do not push, and do not make yourself crazy expecting an overnight change. Let change come to you naturally as you take control of creating your reality.

If you find yourself being overwhelmed by an old undesirable belief during the day, take control again by saying to yourself, "I create my own reality and the present is my point of power."

To get a much more complete description of this process, how and why it works, read *The Nature of Personal Reality: A Seth Book* by Jane Roberts. The process is not magic, you have to work at it a little. But it does work. It is not necessary to accept the details of where or how Roberts came up with it to use the process and benefit from it. It has helped me tremendously to take control of myself and my reality. From personal experience I can attest that you experience what you believe you will experience.

The bottom line is that we can take control of, and responsibility for, our lives. The first step is to pay attention to your mind and thoughts. Second, carve out some quiet time for yourself. Third, inventory and define the various beliefs which compose your belief system. Fourth, recognize that you create your own reality and that the present is your point of power. Finally, structure your beliefs and through them your reality, using the techniques described above.

You do not have to practice these techniques, but even if you decide not to consciously take control and create your reality according to your preferences, you will still create your reality. The present will still be your point of power. The difference is that you will be creating a reality which is based on the "fog" or "psychobabble" of your out-of-control mind. You will have to live with the consequences in either case.

There are short cuts to assist you. Self-help courses, religious groups, training sessions, teachers, and counselors can help expedite the process. If you are inclined to take this process seriously, I suggest reading Stephen Covey's book, *The Seven Habits of Highly Effective People*, which lays out a road map to follow. These are Covey's recommendations:

1. BE PROACTIVE. According to Covey, "as human beings we are responsible for our lives. Our behavior is a function of our decisions, not our conditions." Being proactive, the opposite of reactive, means we have the ability to take the initiative as well as "the responsibility to make things happen."

2. BEGIN WITH THE END IN MIND. In his book, Covey suggests the following exercise: visualize your own funeral and listen as four important people in your life give a eulogy (for example, a relative, a friend, a co-worker, and a member of your church). Consider what you would like each of those speakers to say. Covey asks, "What character would you like them to have seen in you? What contributions, what achievements would you want them to remember? Look carefully at the people around you. What difference would you like to have made in their lives?"

3. PUT FIRST THINGS FIRST. Covey calls this third habit the culmination of the first and second habits. It is, in his words, "the day-in, day-out, moment-by-moment doing it." In another context, recall the Chinese philosopher's advice that a journey of a thousand miles begins with a single step.

4. THINK WIN/WIN. Adam Smith's 18th century principle of interdependence of things economic can be applied to the personal and emotional side of life. According to Covey, the principle of "Win/Win" is based on the paradigm that there is plenty for everyone, and that one person's success

is not achieved at the expense or exclusion of the success of others.

5. SEEK FIRST TO UNDERSTAND, THEN BE UNDERSTOOD. Covey makes the point that we spend most of our lives communicating, that we have undergone extensive training to become effective speakers and writers, but that we often do not know how to listen. Listen first. Understand. Then speak.

6. SYNERGIZE. Synergy "catalyzes, unifies, and unleashes the greatest powers within people," says Covey. Synergy is the culmination of the other habits that enables the whole to be greater than the sum of its parts. It is a state of calm readiness and expectation, allowing a person to recognize, grasp, then utilize opportunity when it appears.

7. SHARPEN THE SAW. This habit is about renewal. According to Covey, there are four ongoing areas in the renewal of self: physical, mental, spiritual, and social/emotional. It is up to us to take care of our most important asset — ourselves. Don't waste or abuse personal resources.

Whether or not you buy Covey's book or any one of another 500 books which can help you on your journey toward self-awareness and self-actualization, the most important advice I can give you is to start by PAYING ATTENTION!!

As you watch and learn from yourself and your environment, you will most likely begin to feel dissatisfied with decisions made by your automatic pilot. Change will become a priority. Although each person may have to address changes in his or her marriage, job, or even church, my focus on change in this book is on politics and money.

First, spend some time and define "enlightened self-interest" for yourself. This would be a good time to review the list of beliefs previously prepared. What is important to you and why? Write down your definition. Reread it at least once a week. Think about it and if necessary, rewrite it. Covey calls this a personal mission statement. It could just as easily be called a personal value system.

Based on your personal mission statement, you will have some idea of what you believe and where you are going. Once the destination is identified, it is easier to decide how to get there.

Next, give some thoughts to these basic principles of action:

GET OUT OF DEBT.

For the purpose of this discussion, there are two kinds of debt, public and private. There is little that can be done about the public debt, until we pay attention to who gets elected and what he or she does in office. We can control private debt. Most of us owe too much. Credit is (or used to be) easy to come by, so we rely on credit when we want (rather than need) something, whether it be a new home or car, a third television, or new clothes.

If you are like the majority of Americans, you are less than ninety days away from being flat broke. If the paychecks stop for an extended period, most of us are unable to maintain the high octane lifestyle we have created for ourselves. In the last several years, bankruptcy filings have soared. Deal with personal debt before you are forced to join the stampede. Follow these simple steps to begin to obtain financial freedom:

1. Keep a record of what you spend. Every penny, including cash and credit spending. Once each month, review the record and notice what you are spending money on, and how much money you are spending.

2. After three months of this, make a budget of what

you should spend. Continue to track your expenditures and compare them to the budget each month. If you are unable to keep to your budget, do not despair, resort to "incrementalism." Re-budget and split the difference to a point which is a little bit closer to your target than your most recent experience. Continue to track expenditures and move ever closer to your budget. As you do this think about these issues: how much money have you earned in your life and what do you have to show for it? Include personal property as well as cash, real estate and cars. What is your net profit each month? Think of yourself as a business and define your personal expenses as a cost of doing business. Is anything left?

3. Take at least part if not all of the money you save as you adhere to your budget and repay debt. Credit cards are a good place to start, since they typically have the highest interest rates. Then move on to car and house payments.

4. Save money. Just a little bit each paycheck will eventually make a big difference in your life. How big? Answer that question by doing the following calculation.

Assume with me that you don't spend $100.00 every two weeks on something or several things which are discretionary in your life, and that you save it instead. After one year you will have $2,400.00. If you can get five percent compounded interest on that for the next fifteen years how much will you have? If you add another $2,400.00 each year for the next fifteen years to that initial deposit, and earn interest on the same terms, then how much will you have? (The answer: you have invested $36,000.00, which swells to $54,378.98 with interest. That is a profit of $18,378.98 which averages to an annual profit of $1,225.26.)

5. Pay cash. It is truly amazing how much more aware of money we become when we pay cash for purchases.

6. Develop a long term financial plan. After experimenting with the foregoing five steps for six or eight months, stop and reassess. You have paid attention to yourself and learned a great deal about your wants and needs, your spending habits and money. You have developed a good understanding of your financial situation. Now you are ready to go farther.

Define your long and short term financial objectives. If you really PAY ATTENTION, if you are frugal and if you are realistic, it is eventually possible to live comfortably on the interest earned from the money you save and invest.

Understand the obstacles and road blocks you will encounter as you work to achieve your objectives. Develop strategies to achieve them. For each strategy adopt one or more specific action plans designed to make the strategy a reality.

BUY QUALITY/BUY AMERICAN.

Most of the time, we really do tend to get what we pay for. There are, of course, rare exceptions and occasional rip-offs. Do not spend money for the sake of spending money — I do not shop at Gucci and I certainly avoid places like Rodeo Drive in Beverly Hills. But I also avoid discounters and outlet stores, because I personally believe we can and often do find a relationship between price and quality. More often than not, we should try to buy American goods and services. It doesn't hurt to do so, and it helps our country. If we buy higher quality merchandise, it almost always lasts longer and works better.

VOTE YOUR POCKETBOOK.

Vote for your economic self-interest. The things that influence people are truly amazing. Please resist voting for youth, charisma, and pretty families. And resist voting for or against someone because of sensational revelations. What in the world did Donna Rice have to do with the kind of job Gary Hart would have done as President? What do we care that Dan Quayle stayed home and served in the National Guard? In both instances, it tells us that these people are human.

The real issue is, "What's in it for me?" OK, so a candidate wants our vote. The candidate can have it if we believe we are more likely than not to benefit from giving it to him or her.

VOTE YOUR FREEDOM.

Any politician who wants to tell us what we can or cannot put into our bodies, what we can or cannot do with our bodies, who we can or cannot sleep, pray, or talk with, what we can or cannot say or read, is a dangerous person and unworthy of our votes. The same can be said for people who like to pin the blame for anything that is wrong with the country on a specific racial, ethnic, or religious group.

These are many variations on the quick fix. Rather than solve a problem, the politician seeks to mandate compliance with an arbitrary standard that will make things "better": ban abortion, or guns, or blame societal problems on a scapegoat like the Blacks, or Jews, or Wasps, or Arabs. Avoid such politicians like the plague. They are on automatic pilot, navigating in fog on a course that leads to disaster. Even worse, they may be cynically manipulating us to gain power. If you think this assessment is wrong, read William Shirer's *The Rise and Fall of the Third Reich* or Edward Gibbon's, *The Decline and Fall of the Roman Empire.*

SAVE TEN PERCENT OF WHAT YOU EARN.

It sounds like a quick fix to say this, but it is not. It is slow and difficult, and terribly easy to ignore. If you do not want to hover ninety days away from destitution, PAY ATTENTION to this idea.

Assume you and your spouse have been in the work force for the last fifteen years. During those years, you have saved next to nothing, yet you have earned (assuming $12,000 each per year = $24,000 x 15 years = $360,000) at least a quarter of a million dollars after taxes. If you followed this rule, you would have $36,000 plus accumulated interest (less taxes) in the bank. If you had put the money into a tax deferred or tax exempt fund, Uncle Sam would also have made a contribution to your savings. Now, in this example, you can survive about one year without government assistance, or you could have paid for a college education for at least one child in advance.

If you say you cannot afford ten percent from the top, take ten percent after taxes. But before you let yourself off so easily, think about it a little more. Can you honestly claim that you have not wasted ten percent of what you have earned? What about those credit card interest payments, or the time payments with interest on installment contracts, or the sexy new car when the old one ran just fine? If you and your spouse are baby boomers, you probably have at least another fifteen years of peak earning potential. It is not too late to implement this program for your benefit. Start today.

REINVENT AMERICA.

We all tend to go along to get along, but that is not good enough any more. We have depended on politicians, business leaders, preachers, and activists to do our thinking for us. You may not have looked around much before reading

179

the first part of this book, but by now you have probably decided that they are not doing a very good job, or you would not still be reading. Our leaders have failed us. It is late in the game, but not too late to salvage something and begin to rebuild.

Hopefully 500,000 people will eventually read this book. Of those, perhaps 5,000 will be motivated to attempt to clean up the various messes they see. The approach detailed in this chapter and the solutions I have recommended to solve problems threatening this country may appeal to as many as one half of those people, or 2,500 folks. Twenty-five hundred motivated, intelligent people who THINK and PAY ATTENTION are simply too few to get the job done unless they recruit others . . . unless they become involved, committed citizens.

We each create our own reality. As we create our personal or individual reality, we contribute to a mass reality. The reality experienced as part of our national life, or our corporate life, or our local or community life is the product of the shared beliefs of the members of each of those organizational subdivisions. This is an automatic process. As we arrive at a belief consensus we will change the daily experience of all Americans far more effectively than any act of Congress or government regulation ever did. We will Reinvent America!

Chapter Eighteen

Our Quality of Life

THE PURPOSE OF THIS BOOK is to define ways in which we can make a positive difference in our life and in the world around us. By using the techniques described below we will no longer have to live life as victims of the whims of others. So let us turn off the automatic pilot and assume full responsibility for improving the quality of our lives.

The hardest thing to do is to get started. If we begin by attempting to change the world overnight, we are bound to fail. Instead, we must do a little at a time. As we experience success in small things, we can expand the program. Eventually, we will find ourselves doing hundreds of "little things" that make positive differences. The impact of these "little things" is cumulative. Before long that cumulative impact will make life significantly better. Be patient. Be persistent.

STEP ONE: MIND

The place to start is with ourselves. Take fifteen to thirty minutes each day. Turn off the phone, television, radio, and stereo, and sit quietly or go for a walk alone. Focus your mind on yourself or your surroundings. Do not think about job or family or problems. Instead focus on something simple like your breathing, or the trees around you, or the clouds above. Pay attention to whatever you have chosen to focus your mind on and exclude all else. This is your quiet time.

Believe it or not, this quiet time is critical to success. If we do nothing else, this alone will improve the quality of our life experience.

There are all kinds of people who can help us learn how to take advantage of this quiet time. People will gladly teach meditation for a small fee, or a priest or minister can provide guidance.

During your quiet time, pay attention to your mind, listen and contemplate. Do not expect any special perceptions. There is no right way to feel, or right sound to hear. Just spend fifteen to thirty minutes in quiet time. Do not prejudice yourself by calling your quiet time meditation or prayer. Do not go into the experience with expectations of any kind.

At some point after this quiet time, review the exercise relating to "beliefs" and take the time to define your beliefs for yourself. These efforts are different but complimentary to your quiet time.

Every day, for a specific few minutes, we must pay attention to ourselves. The benefits are tremendous. It leads to greater intuition and keener insight into personal priorities, both conscious and unconscious. Ultimately, we will enjoy life more.

STEP TWO: BODY

Start getting regular exercise. No matter how busy we are, we can find time to spend an hour every other day in some activity. We do not have to try out for the NFL. Walking, running, working out, playing team sports, going to a gym — it does not matter what, just do it regularly. By the way, those of us who have not recently exercised regularly should get some professional medical or training advice before starting a new regimen.

After we exercise, we can eat more healthful foods and cut down or cut out booze and nicotine. We all know how to feed ourselves and what foods are good for us. If we do not, we can ask someone like a family doctor, or go to the library for information.

Although the primary purpose of this book is political, we cannot be very politically effective if we are hassled, stressed out, unfocused, and cruising toward a stroke or heart attack. The world will not be changed if we fail to pay attention to our spiritual, mental, and physical well-being. By taking care of ourselves, we will feel better, have more fun, feel less stress, meet new friends, live longer, and accomplish more.

STEP THREE: EDUCATION

Take some time to get educated. Each of us, at least once, should go to a political meeting. Try a local Republican or Democratic club, or go to both. Then go to a city council, or a county government meeting. Watch and listen. Ask questions of others present. The most important things to learn include:

These people are people just like you and I, no better and no worse, no smarter or less smart;

these people are involved to gain something which they perceive to be in their best interest;

the system is open to anyone who is willing to take the time and make the effort to influence it;

very few people participate;

very important issues involving lots of dollars and our lifestyles are decided by these people.

183

It is important to actually attend and see this for yourself. Until you do, you will not fully appreciate the truth of the foregoing statements. Just reading them is a poor substitute for seeing and hearing the real thing.

The bottom line on local government is that fortunes are won and lost in these arenas. Lives are changed for better or worse, in areas ranging from the mundane to the esoteric. Where will roads, shopping centers, and crosswalks be built? Which neighborhoods get extra police protection? Who gets garbage picked up once a week, as opposed to twice a week? Where are the schools built? What pot holes get repaired? All of these questions, and more, make a very big difference in our lives, and they are all decided by these people.

The next point to ponder is that no one (or practically no one) pays much attention to who gets elected to these positions of local power, or what they do after they are elected. By becoming active, we can change the course of our local government.

There are three ways to become active. We can participate in the decision about who gets elected, we can focus on the decision-making process by those who are elected and the bureaucrats who serve those elected officials, or we can do both. Your education to this point is not much different than what you can acquire by becoming a college political science student. You might even consider taking a course or two in local government at an educational institution nearby.

Whatever you do to teach yourself about local government, do not take what you learn too seriously. Do not become cannon fodder for one of the political parties or a candidate, do not be seduced into becoming a neighborhood activist, do not become a shill for development interests, and most of all, do not under any circumstances become a true believer. It is important for you to keep your perspective and remain true to your own beliefs.

Tip O'Neill, former Speaker of the United States House of Representatives said, "All politics is local." Once the good, the bad, and the ugly of local politics has been experienced, you are prepared to understand regional, state, and national politics. The process is the same. Only the people and issues vary.

The first stage of this educational process is to gain power. This can be accomplished by winning an election or helping someone else to win an election. It can also be accomplished by working for someone who has already won. A person will have gained power if he or she can determine the agenda of what is to be considered. Power is wielded by those who control the political context (internal to the decision-making body or external to the electorate) in which an issue is considered. It can be accomplished by having the real or perceived power to remove someone from office.

Putting those considerations aside for the moment, the next stage of this education is to develop an understanding of the techniques used to gain and wield power.

The objective here is to show you how to win elections and marshal the resources necessary to gain a majority on any issue which is placed before a deliberative body. Remember, there is no substitute for victory, but no victory is worth sacrificing your character, or compromising your beliefs and ethical standards. The process of politics is surprisingly easy to learn. The teaching mechanism is divided into two parts.

Education Part One: Training

Many organizations will train volunteers, or promise to train them. Both major political parties offer training opportunities, as do many colleges and universities. Most interest groups (regardless of ideology) also offer training.

To train yourself, start by reading *The Prince* by Machiavelli. We should not have to become Machiavellian to effect political change, but it is useful to think about the belief system Machiavelli created. Do you agree with him? Do you believe Machiavelli has defined a "real world" approach to political decision making?

Do you believe it is important to always tell the truth? Do you believe that "good guys" always lose? Are people basically "good" or "bad?" We should not stop asking these kinds of questions until we are truly satisfied that we understand our own value system.

For those who become politically active, each of these beliefs will be tested before long. We will have an easier time if we think about how to deal with situations ahead of time, and consciously decide what we believe before being thrust into the thick of things.

Now, call a local chapter of some group involved in a big fight and volunteer for them. That group could be trying to elect a candidate or promote an issue. A possible problem arising with this approach is that new volunteers are often considered to be expendable and not made privy to the strategic and tactical decision-making that makes or breaks a campaign.

The best group to join is one involved in a close fight which is well financed and not very old. Promotions to positions of leadership in such groups are rapid, whereas stagnant groups will keep new volunteers licking stamps and handing out leaflets. It is important to get into a decision-making capacity where you have the opportunity to make your own mistakes, rather than merely implement someone else's misguided whims.

Another alternative is "Change the World Training," an intensive three-day workshop based on the principles outlined in this book. "Change the World Training" is designed to enable you to take control of your life, to win a campaign, or to wage a battle of influence designed to alter a vote in a legislative or local governing body. This training is comprehensive, based on extensive experience, and calculated to help you become a winner. Please see Appendix E for more information on "Change the World Training."

Education Part Two: Doing

Regardless of how well we have been trained, there is only one way to really internalize that training — just do it! By actually experiencing the "hurley-burley" of the political process, we can gain invaluable knowledge and experience. And, while continuing our education, we can also make a contribution to the political quality of life in the community.

Those of you who choose to participate in the "Change the World Training" program will be placed into a situation in your community, consistent with your beliefs, which will give you the opportunity to actually put your knowledge to work and learn by doing. Those of you not participating in "Change the World Training" should search out an appropriate candidate or issue campaign to volunteer for.

STEP FOUR: THE TEAM

With some on-the-job training behind us, we can take the next step and recruit a team. The political world is, by definition, social. While it is possible to make a difference on an individual basis, individuals will never achieve the results that can be realized by a group of like-minded persons.

There are many ways to recruit a team. Although our

friends, neighbors, co-workers, fellow church members, or even drinking buddies can be enlisted. It is not easy to build a team. People tend to underestimate the difficulties to be encountered, the time required, and antagonisms created by stressful circumstances.

STEP FIVE: OBJECTIVES

Choosing an objective is not as easy as it sounds. Before attainable, realistic objectives can be determined, you must have a thorough understanding of your situation.

Obviously you are dissatisfied with the situation or you would not have taken the time to read this far. Although the focus of this book is broad, being primarily concerned with issues of national scope, your area of concern may be quite different.

You may concern yourself with your children's school and the quality of the education they receive. Or you may be concerned that your city council appears determined to destroy your neighborhood. On the other hand you may want to lower the taxes being collected and spent on education in your school district, or to recapture the county government from the environmental movement. In another context, your hot button might be abortion, the death penalty, preservation of historic buildings, endangered species, or even fluoridation of the water supply. It is your choice.

Let me explain my objective. I believe in the genius of the system created by the Constitution, but I believe that system is being perverted by cynical professionalism. The objective of this book, therefore, is to equip you and others like you with tools you can use to make positive changes in our country and in your life.

First, you must develop a clear understanding of the situation you and your team are confronting. On a single page write a description of the situation that caused you to buy this book in the first place. Consider what you write carefully. It is the foundation for all that follows. Discuss this one-page document with the other members of your team. You must all agree to what is included in the definition of the situation, or you will never succeed.

Second, assemble the team members and write down any objectives that any of you can think of on a large chalk board or butcher paper. This is a brainstorming process that should go on for no more than thirty minutes. Do not discuss the offerings. Do not praise or criticize. Just try to get a full range of possible objectives.

Third, go back to each objective offered and make three lists. The first list should identify the resources (time, people, and money) required to achieve each objective. The second list should contain all of the obstacles to success which could prevent you and your team from succeeding. The third list should itemize the strengths and weaknesses of your team that could make it easier or harder for you to achieve the objective.

Next, set aside the discussion of objectives for awhile and think about the overall mission of your team. This is the most basic issue you must deal with. Begin by thinking about specific objectives for a few minutes to help define the scope of your ambitions. By now you have agreed on the situation in which you find yourselves, and you have considered a wide variety of possible objectives to tackle. You may want to review the situation description to verify that you all still agree it is an accurate description.

What is the difference between a mission and an objective? Why should you bother with a mission statement? The mission defines the boundaries of your team's interest and activities. It says what has to be done and defines how to measure success. For example the mission of the ACLU is to protect civil liberties.

Objectives are more specific, shorter-term goals subsumed within the boundaries defined by the mission. If a mission can be defined as stopping abortion, an objective could be to cut federal aid to abortion clinics.

So, what is your team's mission?

If you define this incorrectly, you will experience frustration and failure. Clear understanding of your mission and acceptance of that mission by all members of the team is paramount, and getting to that agreement may not be as easy as you think. Once the mission is defined and accepted, go back to the objectives you have listed.

Brainstorm possible objectives for another ten minutes. Anything that pertains to the mission should be considered. Put each objective through the process of listing resources, obstacles to success, and pertinent team strengths and weaknesses.

Now, you should finally be ready to pick some objectives. Be prepared to spend a minimum of two to three hours on this, and perhaps two or three days. Consensus is difficult to achieve but well worth the effort.

The objective or objectives should be those which are each necessary to complete the mission and, together, sufficient to assure the team will accomplish its mission. Each objective must be focused on one and only one issue. The word "AND" is absolutely the "kiss of death."

Keep the objectives to a bare minimum. More than four or five is inadvisable. More than eight or ten objectives will almost guarantee failure. If the mission requires more than that number, the mission is too broad for the team and should be reconsidered.

The objectives are those things which MUST be done

to make the team's mission a reality. No more, no less. Again, all members of the team must agree to the objectives if the team is to be successful. It is better to have a small team in full agreement than a larger team in conflict. The team is not a democratic institution, it is more like a family. Each member must agree and be fully committed to each objective. Consensus is crucial.

Now, you must decide how best to achieve the objectives you have agreed upon, by defining those programs necessary to meet each objective. Each program should have a team member who is its owner. The owner is responsible for carrying out the program by a certain date, and within a defined budget. No owner should accept responsibility for more than two or three programs. If you identify too many programs to comply with that rule, go back to the drawing board and think about an additional objective: that of "growth of the team," and various subsidiary programs such as "publicity" or "volunteer recruitment."

By now it should be apparent that this process is one of refinement, moving from a broad concept down to a small, narrowly-defined, specific step. It is time-consuming, but absolutely necessary to ensure that the first step of your thousand mile journey starts in the right direction.

Chapter Nineteen

An End and a Beginning

PROFESSIONALS, WHETHER THEY be elected officials, staff, labor leaders, lobbyists, campaign managers, political consultants, bureaucrats, activists, or journalists, are guilty of throwing our political system out of balance as they serve their own selfish, parochial interests. Each of these professionals has an economic interest in the system as it currently functions.

That economic interest is slowly strangling the system. For example, "Super Lawyers" are helping to sell out our country to the British and Japanese. They are not alone. A massive industry has sprung up to influence government on behalf of various industrial, environmental, ideological, and religious groups with special agendas guaranteed to cost taxpayers more and more.

In the current situation, government and other institutions in society seek to avoid conflict. The status quo has become an end in itself. Our country is becoming stagnant. I believe your injection into the system is necessary to rejuvenate America. Life may not be as cozy for elected and appointed officials, bureaucrats, lawyers, lobbyists, CEOs, and the interests they represent, if you become involved in it.

The major decisions made in this country on a day-to-day basis probably involve between 10,000 and 50,000 people. I want you to become one of the players. Shake up the system. Contribute your ideas, hustle, and sweat. Win or lose, the system and the country will be stronger for the effort you make.

Peter E. Berg, the executive director of Voters of America, a non-profit, non-partisan group, has said "Americans have a deep sense of being shut out of the political system. Americans are NOT apathetic about our government or our political system. They are FRUSTRATED. They want to participate, to have their opinions and concerns listened to, but don't know how."

Voters of America is making it easy for its membership to be heard in Washington. Berg's organization serves as a lobbyist for the interest of the individual. Members jot down their opinions on pending legislation and send them to Voters of America. Letters representing compiled, summarized viewpoints of organization members are sent to the Congresspersons and Senators who are representatives of those Voters of America members. Copies of these letters are also furnished to the leadership in Congress, who promote the points of view favored by Voters of America members. Letters are always accompanied by a list of names and addresses of those individual Voters of America members supporting the points made in the letter, along with a summary of comments made by those individuals.

Voters of America also arranges for Congressional representatives to personally take phone calls from its members via a toll-free telephone bank. People can talk to real decision makers person-to-person, without having to hire a lawyer, lobbyist, or PR firm to intervene.

To find out more about Voters of America, write Peter Berg at 601 Pennsylvania Avenue N.W., Washington, D.C. 20004.

The ultimate solution is to change the nature of the game by changing the players, as the Voters of America organization is doing. If enough people become adept at using the tools previously reserved to the professional, those professionals will lose part of their clout with government. Elected officials and bureaucrats will no longer be able to isolate themselves from their real constituencies, while building cozy relationships with organizations with whom they hope to obtain future employment. They will be forced to respond and serve the taxpayers who pay their salaries. Ultimately, the reality of government will change, returning to a condition somewhat closer to what our founders intended.

Of course I believe that the policy changes I put forth in earlier chapters make sense and that you should support my ideas. But, even if you think I am wrong and just avail yourself of "Change the World" training to put forth your own concept of what is right, you will have the desired effect. This new activism will not solve all of the problems with government overnight, but it will improve the situation slowly over time.

The preceding analysis explains why I do not particularly care what your objectives are or whether I agree with them, and why it is important that you choose objectives which are attainable, realistic, and meaningful to you. You will win some battles and lose others. But, your mere presence in the game will change it. It will no longer be possible to just "go along to get along." It will not be as convenient to avoid dealing with issues, or as easy to confuse the self-interest of the government official, and his or her professional "friends," with our best interests as a people.

You can make a difference. Starting with yourself and working outward to family, friends, neighbors, co-workers, and fellow citizens, you can "change the world."

The best example I can give as proof of my point is Ernest Cortes, Jr., and the Industrial Areas Foundation established by Saul Alinsky. The foundation represents 1.5 million families and is based on the idea that people who are angry over poverty, injustice, or benign neglect can use their anger as a positive force. That anger brings people together in a process known as an "action," a meeting during which a person in power is confronted about an issue. The issue must be specific, concrete, and winnable. Rather than a broad concept, such as the "education problem" or the "drug problem," an issue could be something like poor police protection for a neighborhood, which results in a flourishing drug market. Participants in the "action" have specific solutions to suggest to the person in power. By the way, the person in power need not be an elected official, it could as easily be a school principal, business owner, or bureaucrat.

Cortes founded a Texas affiliate of Alinsky's Industrial Areas Foundation in 1974, known as Communities Organized for Public Service. Former San Antonio Mayor Henry Cisneros claims it has set the moral and political tone of San Antonio. After a dozen years of effort by this group, 750 million dollars has been invested in infrastructure in the poorest areas of the city. People can and do change the world.

You are limited only by yourself. Remember, you create your own reality and the present is your point of power. What are you waiting for?

Epilogue

Regardless of whether the solutions described in this book will work or even be given the chance to succeed, the process I have described is correct. I view the problems confronting America in the context of the system; any solutions must begin with the smallest, most important unit of the system — the individual. Injecting new blood in the form of new players into the system will provide the best chance to Reinvent America.

You are the key, will you put down this book and forget it? Or will you begin to take control of your life and your country? I believe that like me, most of you are madder than hell about what is happening to our country and are unwilling to be couch potatoes, watching the decline and fall of America. So use your common sense. Figure out what makes you most uncomfortable and join us on the field. Be a player. Together, we will Reinvent America.

The End

Reinventing America
Appendices

Appendix A
Excerpts from *The Wealth of Nations* by Adam Smith
(Penguin Group, London, England, 1986)

Every man is rich or poor according to the degree in which he can afford to enjoy the necessaries, conveniences, the amusements of human life. But after the division of labor has once thoroughly taken place, it is but a very small part of these with which a man's own labor can supply him. The far greater of them he must derive from the labor of other people, and he must be rich or poor according to the quantity of that labor which he can command, or which he can afford to purchase. The value of any commodity, therefore, to the person who possesses it and who means not to use it for himself, but to exchange it for other commodities, is equal to the quantity of labor which it enables him to purchase or command. Labor, therefore, is the real measure of the exchangeable value of all commodities.

The real price of everything, what everything really costs to the man who wants to acquire it, is the toil and trouble of acquiring it. What everything is really worth to the man who has acquired it, and who wants to dispose of it or exchange it for something else, is the toil and trouble which it can save to himself and which it can impose upon other people.

When the price of any commodity is neither more nor less than what is sufficient to pay the rent of the land, the wages of the labor, and the profits of the stock employed in raising, preparing and bringing it to market, according to their natural rates, the commodity is then sold for what may be called its natural price.

The commodity is then sold precisely for what it is worth, or for what it really cost the person who brings it to market; for though in common language what is called the prime cost of any commodity does not comprehend the profit of the person who is to sell it again, yet if he would sell it at a price which does not allow him the ordinary rate of profit in his neighborhood, he is evidently a loser by the trades: since by employing his stock in some other way he might have made a profit.

The actual price at which any commodity is commonly sold is called its market price. It may either be above, or below, or exactly the same with its natural price.

The market price of every particular commodity is regulated by the proportion between the quantity which is actually brought to the market, and the demand of those who are willing to pay the natural price of the commodity, or the whole value of the rent, labor, and profit, which must be paid in order to bring it to market.

The quantity of every commodity brought to market naturally suits itself to the effectual demand. It is the interest of all those who employ their land, labor, or stock, in bringing any commodity to market that the quantity never should exceed the actual demand; and it is the interest of all other people that it never should fall short of that demand.

The natural price, therefore, is, as it were, the central price, to which the price of all commodities are continually gravitating.

The market price of any particular commodity, though it may continue long above, can seldom continue long below its natural price. Whatever part of it was paid below the natural rate, the person whose interest it effected would immediately feel the loss, and would immediately withdraw either so much land, or so much labor, or so much stock, from being employed about it, that the quantity brought to market would soon be no more than sufficient as to supply the effectual demand. It's market price, therefore, would soon rise to the natural price. *This at least would be the case where there was perfect liberty.*

[No economic endeavor] puts into motion a greater quantity than that of the farmer. Not only is laboring servants, but as laboring cattle, are productive laborers. In agriculture, too, nature labors along with man; and though her labor costs no expense, his produce has its value, as well as that of the most expensive workmen. The most important operations agriculture same intended not so much to increase, though they do that too, as to direct the fertility of nature towards the production of the plants most profitable to man....It is the work of nature which remains after inducting or compensating everything which can be regarded as the work of man. It is seldom less than a fourth, and frequently more than a third of the whole produce. No equal quantity of productive labor employed in manufacturers can ever occasion so great reproduction....The capital employed in agriculture, therefore, not only puts into motion a greater quantity of productive labor than any equal capital employed in manufacturers, but in proportion, too, to the quantity of productive labor, which it employs, it adds a much greater value to the annual produce of the land and labor of the country, to the real wealth and revenue of its inhabitants. Of all the ways in which a capital can be employed, it is by far the most advantageous to the society.

There is one sort of labor which adds to the value of the subject on which it is bestowed; there is another which has no such effect. The former, as it produces a value, may be called productive; the latter, unproductive. Thus the labor of a manufacturer adds, generally to the value of the materials which she works upon, that of his own maintenance and of his master's profit. The labor of a menial servant, on the contrary adds to the value of nothing....A man grows rich by employing a multitude of manufacturers; he grows poor by maintaining a multitude of menial servants.

The labor of some of the most respected orders in the society is, like that of menial servants, unproductive of any value and does not fix or realize itself in any permanent subject, or vendable commodity, which endures after the labor is passed, and for which an equal quantity of labor could afterwards be procured. The sovereign, for example, with all the officers both of justice and war who serve under him, the whole Army and Navy, are unproductive laborers. They are the servants of the public, and are maintained by part of the annual produce of other people. Their service, how honorable, how useful, or how necessary so ever, produces nothing for which an equal quantity of service can afterwards be procured. The protection, security and defense of the commonwealth, the effect of their labor this year, will not purchase its protection, security, and defense for the year to come. In the same class must be ranked some of the greatest and most important, and most frivolous professions; churchmen, lawyers, physicians, men of letters of all kinds; players, buffoons, musicians, opera-singers, opera-dancers, etc. The labor of the meanest of these has a certain value, regulated by the very same principles which regulate every other sort of labor; and that of the noblest and most useful produces nothing which could afterwards purchase or procure an equal quantity of labor. Like the declamation of the actor, the harangue of the orator, or the tune of the musician, the work of all of them perishes at the very instant of its production.

Both productive and unproductive labors and those who do not labor at all, are all equally maintained by the annual produce of the land and the country. This produce, how great soever, can never be infinite, but must have certain limits.

Great nations are never impoverished by private, they sometimes are by public illegality and misconduct. The whole, or almost the whole public revenue, is in most countries employed in maintaining unproductive hands. Such are the people who compose a numerous and splendid court, a great ecclesiastical establishment, great fleets and armies, who in time of peace produce nothing, in time of war acquire nothing, which can compensate the expense of maintaining them, even while the war lasts. Such people as they themselves produce nothing, are all maintained by the produce of other men's labor. While multiplied, therefore, to an unnecessary number, they may in a particular year consume so great a share in this produce, as not to leave a sufficiency for maintaining the productive laborers who should reproduce it next year. The next year's produce will, therefore, be less than that of the foregoing, and if the same disorder should continue, that of the third year will be still less of the second. Those unproductive hands, who should be maintained by a part only of the spare revenue of the people, may consume so great a share of the whole revenue, and thereby oblige so great a number to encroach upon of their capital, upon the funds destined for the maintenance of productive labor, that all the frugality and good conduct of individuals may not be able to compensate the waste and degradation of produce occasioned by this violent and enforced encroachment.

The price of monopoly is upon every occasion the highest which can be got. The natural price, or the price of free competition, on the contrary, is the lowest which can be taken, not upon every occasion, indeed, but for any consideration time together. The one is upon every occasion the highest which can be squeezed out of the buyers, or which, it is supposed, they will consent to give: the other is the lowest which the sellers can commonly afford to take, and at the same time continue their business.

The exclusive privileges of corporations, statutes of apprenticeship, and all those laws which restrain, in particular employment, the competition to a smaller number than might otherwise go into them, have the same tendency, though in a less degree. They are a sort of enlarged monopolies, and they frequently, for ages together, and in whole classes of employment, keep up the market price of particular commodities above the natural price, and maintain both wages of labor and the profits of the stock employed about them somewhat above their natural rate.

Such enhancements in the market price may last as long as the regulations of police which give occasion to them.

Appendices

Appendix B
Interview with Carl H. Wilken
excerpted from Unforgiven by Charles Walters, Jr.
(Economic Library, Kansas City, MO, 1971)

WALTERS. In your published statements, you and your associates made reference to a trade turn or multiplier. According to these findings, you say that national income is nothing more than raw material income times (5), or farm income times (7). What in fact governs this ratio or trade turn?

WILKEN: It starts with efficiency. Going back to 1787, some nine out of ten people were farmers. But by 1850 only half the people were farming and mining and so on. So the trade turn moved up to 2 - or one farmer was required to feed two people. In the 1910-1914 period, the turn came to about 5. If the trade turn is computed in terms of all raw materials, that ratio still holds today. If you compute earned national income on the basis of farm income, then the ratio is 7. To illustrate the point - from 1920 to 1933 gross farm income fell off $6.8 billion, and the national income fell $47.6 billion, or $7 of national income was lost for every dollar of farm income lost. This ratio still holds. In 1945, when the farmer got $14.2 billion net income, it was a trade turn of 7.01. From 1928 to 1953, the trade turn averaged 7.04. In other words, for a ten year period that involved both war years and a post-war period - and when we had 90% price supports for basic farm crops - the trade turn proved out at $6.97 of national income for every dollar of farm income. Now agricultural income has continued to turn out an earned income on the ratio of approximately 7, but this is hardly half enough income to operate the economy. I call this a shortage. The rest of the income - the unearned income - has been developed by injecting borrowed money into the economy. Between 1951 [and] 1964 the national economy sustained an operating loss of $3,300 billion. This happens to duplicate what happened between 1929 and 1942, when we lost $563 billion of income because we didn't maintain the 1929 price level on farm products. During the depression years we absorbed the loss by doing without $463 billion of goods. During that period, also, we started with the Keynesian theory and government programs, but by not getting farm income back up to the appropriate level, we simply liquidated just about as much private debt between 1929 and 1940 as we added to federal debt through government programs. The total debt at the end of 1940 was almost exactly the same as it was in 1929. It was not until 1941, when our income got back to the 1929 level, that the 12 central states got back to the 1929 income level.

WALTERS. When you say earned income and income generated by debt, exactly what do you mean?

WILKEN. It takes about $5.50 of national income to pay $1.00 interest made necessary by capital debt creation. Don't confuse this with operating debt. You see, the idea behind the Fed was that money could be created and extinguished when the crop came in. when you borrow to put in a crop or stock inventory, you have what amounts to a floor plan debt. It has to be paid off as soon as the crop is in or the merchandise sold. The lending institution has a claim against income generated this way, and it has that claim first. In other words, the bank takes repayment for the loan off the top. I'm not talking about that kind of debt. I'm talking about capital debt - the kind of debt that is being injected into this economy because income has been

202

short due to underpayment to agriculture. An economy can only expand its production facilities, or its capital investment, out of profit. It cannot borrow capital beyond its ability to generate profits to pay it off. Operating debt has to be paid on an as-you-go basis. So do expenses and other costs in doing business. This means capital has to come out of profits, and repayment of capital debt has to come out of profits. And interest has to be paid out of profits. Now here is what is happening. By injecting debt into the economy - capital debt - the nation manages to earn about $5 of national income for every dollar of new capital debt. That's income generated by debt. But it takes about $5.50 of national income to generate a single dollar of profit with which to either pay interest or liquidate any part of that capital debt. As a result, we now [circa 1967] have over $1.5 trillion public and private debt, and it will be very near $2 trillion* by the end of the decade. At 7% interest. The thing that's wrong with income generated by debt is that it cannot be paid, and eventually it cannot be carried. That's the situation in the country right now.

WALTERS. Within this framework, what is the situation in farming?

WILKEN. About the same. Halfway through the 60s, in spite of all the prosperity you hear about, this economy lacked $73 billion of having enough income to balance with wages and interest. Some $68 billion of that was the shortage of income for farm operators, farm business, and corporate profit after taxes. Without earned income, here's what happens. A young man inherits a farm or business. He goes out, he wants to expand to stay even, so he borrows some money, and then he borrows some more. Pretty soon he's in over his head, and he can't borrow enough to cover the interest on the loans as they fall due. Finally he loses the entire business. That's what we're doing to the United States.

WALTERS. Does this multiplier you call a trade turn prevail in all economies? Does it hold in the Russian socialist economy, for instance?

WILKEN. They all have a trade turn, but they all have different trade turns. In Russia, I believe they have a trade turn of about 2.

WALTERS. What accounts for the difference?

WILKEN. Efficiency of agricultural production, basically. We talk a lot about efficiency - farm efficiency and labor efficiency. Well, most of our labor efficiency is brought about by capital investment in machines. In other words, the average workman in a factory works less in terms of physical energy than he did 20 years ago. Labor organizations have taken this machine efficiency and bargained it into twice as much increase as labor is entitled to receive. On the other hand, agriculture - because of its efficiency, machine efficiency included - has been penalized with a reduction in prices. When agriculture produces enough to release a man to work in another field, the trade turn goes up. Now to illustrate this: in 1787 one out of every ten people in the country were farmers, and it was farmers who drafted the Constitution of the United States. I don't think the present group of intellectuals could draft

---

* Gross public and private debt came to $1.9351 trillion by the end of the decade (1970), or $44.9 billion short of Wilken's off-hand estimate.

a constitution equal to the one our forebears drafted**. Nowadays, they've got too many theories involved. They haven't got the practical common sense and down-to-earth thinking to write a constitution. The Constitution of the United States is a wonderful document. And the whole economy is tied up in Article 1, Section 8, in which Congress was given the right to establish a monetary system and to issue money, which became the dollar, and to regulate the value thereof, which is price. And - also- to protect it with import duties, or whatever it might take. This is the same article that gives Congress the right and duty to regulate weights and measures. This is significant. In Europe, they set up the metric system. Well, in the first session of Congress they set up our weights and measures systems, and our money system. They had two purposes in mind. One, to start to protect the development of industry in the United States. Two, to maintain the value of money and to run the government. At first we supported the federal government with import fees and two excise taxes. From 1797 we ran the government that way. In 1914 we brought in the income tax. To illustrate: in 1910 it took $680 million to operate the government of the United States. In 1966 it took $137 billion. Well, where are these additional dollars going to come from? There are only two sources. One is production, and the second is the price of that production. In 1789 we passed a sugar tariff. At that time it was 2 cents a pound. At 2 cents a pound with wages at about 50 cents a day, it was a pretty high tariff. Why? We wanted sugar. We wanted to bring about domestic sugar production. And we've had support prices for sugar ever since. We have it today. Our price is usually double the world price.

WALTERS. When did the development of American agriculture start to deliver a trade turn of more than 1 for 1?

WILKEN. About 1850. At that time we had developed our resources to the point where we could release one man to go into other lines of endeavor. We had a 2 times trade turn.

WALTERS. What was the multiplier, or trade turn, around the pre-World War I era?

WILKEN. In the 1910-1914 period, we had a trade turn of about 4.5 to 1. In short the national income was about 4.5 times bigger than the gross farm income. It was during this period that we brought in most of the big machinery on farms. We brought in the horse-drawn gang plow, the horse drawn eight foot binder, all big equipment. We developed the harvesting of grain by running it through a binder and tying it in bundles. We developed the threshing machine. It was moving fast. By 1921, and until 1953, the trade turn in terms of agriculture reached 7.

WALTERS. I understand, according to your calculations, that this trade turn has pretty much stabilized itself since that time.

WILKEN. Well, in 1929 we had $87.8 billion of national income and we had $13.9 billion of gross farm income. In making calculation, you have to be careful to

---

** Rexford G. Tugwell, a former New Deal Brain truster, has written a 10,000 word, 11 article model under the auspices of the Center for the Study of Democratic Institutions. It recommends a single term for the president, life terms for Senators, and republics to take over the states. Tugwell was quoted by Wall Street Journal, September 9, 1970, as characterizing the old constitution as "primitive in the extreme."

use the gross realized farm income figure. You see, there are half a dozen different kinds of farm income, according to the statisticians. Now in 1933 the gross farm income was $7.1 billion. If you subtract that from $13.9 billion, you'll have a drop of 6.8 billion. According to the economic theories, that kind of a drop would have been a great benefit because if made food cheaper, and people presumably could buy more. That's the supply and demand idea, but it does not take into account how income is created in the first place. You have an illustration of how it works in the records. When that farm income drop took place, national income dropped from $87.8 billion down to $40.2 billion, a drop of $47.6 billion. If you'll divide the $6.8 billion into $47.6, you'll find how we get this 7 times ratio. Remember, because of low payment to agriculture, we continued to lose national income all through the depression and through 1940. Then in the pickup from 1940 to 1943, we increased our gross farm income $11 billion to $23.4 billion, and we increased our national income seven times that amount from $81.6 billion to $170.3 billion. That's how the depression ended. The survival of the nation required stabilization of the economy. We did it in one year because a war threatened survival of the system. We could have done it without a war just as well.

WALTERS. This cause and effect relationship between income at the farm level and the national level - can you prove that it is more than just a ratio that might be happenstance?

WILKEN. Look - the aim of all science is to predict. When we get enough evidence together to predict, we join the observations together into working relationships called laws. These laws enable men not only to predict, but to design the outcome. Cause and effect, natural or managed, must be understood. This goes back to earned income, and draws a distinction between it and income that pretends to be earned. Now Kansas City has a Federal Reserve Bank. If you'll go to the Federal Reserve Bank there and get the bank turns from 1929 to 1932 you'll really get an eye opener. It will prove to you that your bank turns dropped in direct proportion to the drop in the value of farm production and income level.

WALTERS. But they're not doing that now?

WILKEN. They're not doing that now because of injection of borrowed money.

WALTERS. In other words, to keep the national level from dipping in harmony with the farm level, we've injected credit to keep the economic kite flying?

WILKEN. Right. For every dollar income you've increased in the last six years, you've added $2 to your debt.

WALTERS. You say the income is created, but the mounting debt is still owed. But the Keynesian economists say, "So what, we owe it to ourselves."

WILKEN. That's the trouble. Let's just take the debt that we've added since 1950. If you'll take a lead pencil and figure 5% interest, that's $50 billion interest that has to be paid on $1 trillion. Now you have a 20% operating profit for the United States as a whole, so it takes well over $5 of national income to generate $1 of profit to pay that interest. We may owe it to ourselves, but ourselves is really a few millionaires.

WALTERS. What you're describing here is a geometrical progression. You'd be doubling this debt in a decade and doubling it just on the basis of interest. Can anything - people, hummingbirds or debt - stand geometric redoubling?

205

WILKEN. Absolutely not. Let me illustrate this thing. In 1929 we had $214 billion gross debt, federal, state, local and private. In 1940, after 11 years of operation, we had $215 billion. In other words, practically no increase in the total debt. Now the private debt had been reduced through liquidation, repudiation, foreclosure, but in carrying on the New Deal policies we injected almost an equivalent amount of federal debt. We created new debt about as fast as we repudiated or liquidated the old, and we got nowhere. In this period we lost $563 billion dollars of income, or roughly 7 times the underpayment for farm products below the 1929 level. How did we absorb this loss? We went without the goods that $563 billion would have purchased at the 1929 price level. That was during the depression. This time we've done things differently. Since the end of 1950 we have lost $7 of the national income that should have been earned, or 7 times the underpayment to agriculture. But to offset it we've poured in this additional debt. And we've used the backward roll of this money to offset the loss in income. We've called it prosperity.

WALTERS. The nation's profit is determined, according to what you're describing here, by the valuation you put on raw materials at the beginning of each cycle?

WILKEN. That's right. Then you end up in this position. It takes $250 billion of income in 1967 to earn the interest on the debt expansion from the end of 1950 to 1967. Saying it another way - if we didn't have this $1 trillion additional debt in 1967, we could operate the United States with $250 billion less income during the year.

WALTERS. Could you set up a table showing - say from 1920 to the present - that the money paid for farm raw materials, oil, shale, stone, lumber and other raw materials became the earned income (that is, the income not created by debt injection), and then make a projection to illustrate exactly how much debt creation became mandatory in order to sustain the national income at a socially acceptable level?

WILKEN. That could be done, surely.

WALTERS. Is the information the government makes available suitable for easy translation into such a table?

WILKEN. Not at all. In my publication. All New Wealth Comes From the Soil, I tabulated the record of all raw material income from 1929 to 1953. To finish the table from 1948 to 1953, I had to send a special request to the Bureau of Mines for tabulations on mineral raw material income so that it would be expressed the same as it had been in 1948. In 1948 they discontinued the tabulation on metals recovered by smelting or recycling and translated the figures into manufactured income.

WALTERS. Why did they do that?

WILKEN. Well, it made manufacturing income look bigger, and helped make corporations look capable of paying bargained wages. In any case, I got a special statement from the Bureau of Mines finishing the period I was interested in. In that period your value of farm production plus your other raw materials were equal to 95% of the profit in operating the United States. Now what happened to the other 5%. The other 5% was standing expansion. That's where you got your money to expand.

WALTERS. But this table could be brought up to date?

WILKEN. With revised figures, yes. You see, you have to start with raw materials. What do you do with a ton of ore? You fabricate it into different parts. But you don't add one ton of ore. You don't add one pound. You do add value in terms of dollars, because of the capital cost factor in transporting and in paying processing labor, and so on, and all this is added on to the raw material, finally ending in your consumer price level. Let's take the full raw material equation. The record proves you have a five times turn. You have the initial dollars of raw materials. Now through your system of private enterprise, you carry this thing through, transportation, processing, and so on. What does private enterprise have to do to accomplish all this? It has to borrow the money - the operating account to pay for the cost of transportation, to pay for processing, to pay labor cost, to pay return on capital and that value in terms of dollars is added to the consumer price. And it is sold at the consumer level.

Appendices

Appendix C
excerpt from *Raw Materials Economics* by
Charles Walters Jr.
(Acres U.S.A., Kansas City, MO, 1991)

Long reliant upon raw-material prices that are too low to support a true prosperity, the American economy cannot restore itself through free market forces alone. This is because the free market system today does not function due to the concentrated power of raw material marketing conglomerates. In order to put the economy back on the right track we must enact a new law.

The proposed National Economic Stability Act (NESA) is such a law. Simply stated, this proposed legislation would establish a price structure for basic storable commodities harvested off 75 to 80% of America's tillable acres. It would also regulate the parity values at which semi-storable commodities—potatoes, meat and dairy animal products—could enter trade channels. Once this production is priced correctly, values of perishable produce and other raw materials would fall in line, laying the foundation for stability and prosperity unlimited.

1. NESA eliminates current federal crop subsidy, financing, and commodity buying programs. Since NESA will establish a new and truly fair market, continued government intervention will be unnecessary. Government may purchase food for such programs as foreign aid and school lunches, but it must buy all such commodities on the open market and pay the same price as other buyers.

2. Prices for storable foodstuffs and fiber (corn, wheat, barley, oats, soybeans, rice, cotton, potatoes, milo) and for livestock, dairy animals and poultry will be set at a minimum of 90% of parity and a maximum of 115% of parity. These prices will be based on USDA figures drawn from the 1910-1914 base period, and they may fluctuate within the limits as the market demands. To ensure uniformity, the Consumer Price Index and the Wholesale Price Index will also be reset to fit the parity price structure.

3. The minimum wage equals the parity price of a bushel of corn. This feature ensures the adjustment of the whole economy to the new price structure for primary supply products, and it guarantees mass purchasing power sufficient to absorb the supply of those products at the new market prices.

4. Agricultural producers may plant the crops they wish in the amount they wish, but they can sell only what the domestic and export markets will absorb. Production-for-sale quotas for each producer will be authorized by marketing certificates issued annually.

5. Excess product (i.e., over the amount allowed by the marketing certificate) must be stored at the producer's expense. The stored product will provide an important hedge against bad weather and crop failure. Also, it can provide the basis for establishing a national food and fiber reserve, which would greatly strengthen the nation's defense. This provision distinguishes NESA from the current parity pricing law for milk, which encourages overproduction by obligating the government to buy excess production no matter how much it exceeds actual demand.

6. Imports of the products governed by NESA must be priced domestically at 110% parity. This provision is needed to prevent the domestic market from being flooded by cheap commodities from abroad. Ultimately, too, NESA will work to the benefit of raw materials producers overseas, by guaranteeing them a fair and

adequate price for their products and thereby establishing their economies on the firm foundation needed for sound economic development.

Implementing NESA requires only a simple organizational structure, one that gives agricultural producers a major voice and that trims governmental involvement to the minimum necessary to ensure efficient and impartial administration.

Prices for regulated commodities will be set monthly for each Farm Credit District by the USDA under the supervision of the National Board of Producers. The Board, chaired by the Secretary of Agriculture, will be elected by producers of the covered commodities. Each Farm Credit District will elect one member. Every county and state agriculture department will be advised by similar producer boards conprising three regular delegates and two alternates, all of whom must be producers of one or more basic commodities.

It will be the responsibility of the National Board to establish domestic and foreign demand before the production season begins and to update these figures every quarter. The Board will also issue marketing certificates and update them quarterly. Certificates will be based on the production history of each grower, with allowances made for new and retiring producers as needed. If the National Board finds that demand falls below select year production levels, the shares of larger than average producers will be fractioned downward.

To ensure compliance with NESA's regulations, sellers and buyers must report first-entry-to-market transactions to the county ASCS office on a monthly basis. This requirement also covers co-ops, which are allowed to store, process, and market all members' produce covered by marketing certificates. Covered production may also be used as collateral for loans.

Contractors who buy or sell at prices above or below the set levels will be fined three times the dollar amount of the transaction. Fraud, including selling without a marketing certificate, will be subject to other legal penalties.

A commodity tax will be levied on each covered commodity upon first entry to the market. The amount of the tax will be computed to cover the cost of administering the program plus commodity marketing promotion and production research. The tax is to be included as an expense in the parity formula, so that domestic and foreign consumers and buyers will be contributing to the programs.

In keeping with NESA's self-sufficiency, all CCC loans will be transferred to private banks and financial institutions, and all federal programs governing the commodities regulated by NESA will be suspended. Likewise, special concessions granted to corporations engaged in productive agriculture will be suspended. In short, agricultural subsidies for the affected commodities will end.

If this economic policy is to succeed, it must aim at the root cause of the current malaise: primary supply price depression. A new policy focus is needed.

The health of the primary supply sector determines the health of the whole economy. Revitalizing the primary supply means increasing net income. And that means equitable raw materials prices.

Appendices

Appendix D
The Declaration of Independence
IN CONGRESS, JULY 4, 1776

The Unanimous Declaration of the Thirteen United States of America

When in the course of human events, it becomes necessary for one people to dissolve the political bands which have connected them with another, and to assume among the powers of the earth, the separate and equal station to which the laws of Nature and of Nature's God entitle them, a decent respect to the opinions of mankind requires that they should declare the causes which impel them to the separation.

We hold these truths to be self-evident, that all men are created equal, that they are endowed by their Creator with certain unalienable rights, that among these are life, liberty and the pursuit of happiness. That to secure these rights, governments are instituted among men, deriving their just powers from the consent of the governed- That whenever any form of government becomes destructive of these ends, it is the right of the people to alter or to abolish it, and to institute new government, laying its foundation on such principles and organizing its powers in such form, as to them shall seem most likely to effect their safety and happiness. Prudence, indeed, will dictate that governments long established should not be changed for light and transient causes; and accordingly all experience hath shown, that mankind are more disposed to suffer, while evils are sufferable, than to right themselves by abolishing the forms to which they are accustomed. But when a long train of abuses and usurpations, pursuing invariably the same object evinces a design to reduce them under absolute despotism, it is their right, it is their duty, to throw off such government, and to provide new guards for their future security. Such has been the patient sufferance of these Colonies; and such is now the necessity which constrains them to alter their former systems of government. The history of the present King of Great Britain is a history of repeated injuries and usurpations, all having in direct object the establishment of an absolute tyranny over these States. To prove this, let facts be submitted to a candid world.

He has refused his assent to laws, the most wholesome and necessary for the public good. He has forbidden his Governors to pass laws of immediate and pressing importance, unless suspended in their operation till his assent should be obtained; and when so suspended, he has utterly neglected to attend to them. He has refused to pass other laws for the accommodation of large districts of people, unless those people would relinquish the right of representation in the legislature, a right inestimable to them and formidable to tyrants only.

He has called together legislative bodies at places unusual, uncomfortable, and distant from the depository of their public records, for the sole purpose of fatiguing them into compliance with his measures.

He has dissolved Representative Houses repeatedly, for opposing with manly firmness his invasions on the rights of the people.

He has refused for a long time, after such dissolutions, to cause others to be elected; whereby the legislative powers, incapable of annihilation, have returned to the people at large for their exercise; the State remaining in the mean time exposed to all the dangers of invasion from without, and convulsions within.

He has endeavoured to prevent the population of these States; for that purpose obstructing the laws for naturalization of foreigners; refusing to pass others to

210

encourage their migrations hither, and raising the conditions of new appropriations of lands.

He has obstructed the administration of justice, by refusing his assent to laws for establishing judiciary powers.

He has made judges dependent on his will alone, for the tenure of their offices, and the amount and payment of their salaries.

He has erected a multitude of new offices, and sent hither swarms of officers to harass our people, and eat out their substance.

He has kept among us, in times of peace, standing armies without the consent of our legislatures.

He has affected to render the military independent of and superior to the civil power.

He has combined with others to subject us to a jurisdiction foreign to our constitution, and unacknowledged by our laws; giving his assent to their acts of pretended legislation:

For quartering large bodies of armed troops among us:

For protecting them, by a mock trial, from punishment for any murders which they should commit on the inhabitants of these States: For cutting off our trade with all parts of the world:

For imposing taxes on us without our consent:

For depriving us in many cases, of the benefits of trial by jury:

For transporting us beyond seas to be tried for pretended offenses:

For abolishing the free system of English laws in a neighbouring province, establishing therein an arbitrary government, and enlarging its boundaries so as to render it at once an example and fit instrument for introducing the same absolute rule into these colonies: For taking away our charters, abolishing our most valuable laws, and altering fundamentally the forms of our governments:

For suspending our own legislatures, and declaring themselves invested with power to legislate for us in all cases whatsoever.

He has abdicated government here, by declaring us out of his protection and waging war against us.

He has plundered our seas, ravaged our coasts, burnt our towns, and destroyed the lives of our people.

He is at this time transporting large armies of foreign mercenaries to complete the works of death, desolation and tyranny, already begun with circumstances of cruelty and perfidy scarcely paralleled in the most barbarous ages, and totally unworthy of the head of a civilized nation.

He has constrained our fellow citizens taken captive on the high seas to bear arms against their country, to become the executioners of their friends and brethren, or to fall themselves by their hands.

He has excited domestic insurrections amongst us, and has endeavoured to bring on the inhabitants of our frontiers, the merciless Indian savages, whose known rule of warfare is an undistinguished destruction of all ages, sexes and conditions.

In every stage of these oppressions we have petitioned for redress in the most humble terms: Our repeated petitions have been answered only by repeated injury. A prince, whose character is thus marked by every act which may define a tyrant, is unfit to be the ruler of a free people.

Nor have we been wanting in attentions to our British brethren. We have warned them from time to time of attempts by their legislature to extend an unwarrantable jurisdiction over us. We have reminded them of the circumstances of our emigration and settlement here. We have appealed to their native justice and magnanimity, and we have conjured them by the ties of our common kindred to disavow these usurpations, which, would inevitably interrupt our connections and correspondence. They too have been deaf to the voice of justice and of consanguinity. We must, therefore, acquiesce in the necessity which denounces our separation, and hold them, as we hold the rest of mankind, enemies in war, in peace friends.

WE, THEREFORE, the Representatives of the United States of America, in General Congress, Assembled, appealing to the Supreme Judge of the world for the rectitude of out intentions, do, in the name, and by authority of the good people of these Colonies, solemnly publish and declare, That these United Colonies are, and of right ought to be FREE AND INDEPENDENT STATES; that they are absolved from all allegiance to the British Crown, and that all political connection between them and the State of Great Britain, is and ought to be totally dissolved; and that as free and independent States, they have full power to levy war, conclude peace, contract alliances, establish commerce, and to do all other acts and things which independent States may of right do. And for the support of this Declaration, with a firm reliance on the protection of Divine Providence, we mutually pledge to each other our lives, our fortunes and our sacred honor.

(Signers)

Appendix D (cont.)
The Constitution of the United States of America

PREAMBLE

WE THE PEOPLE of the United States, in order to form a more perfect Union, establish justice, insure domestic tranquility, provide for the common defense, promote the general welfare, and secure the blessings of liberty to ourselves and our posterity, do ordain and establish this Constitution for the United States of America.

ARTICLE I

SECTION 1. All legislative powers herein granted shall be vested in a Congress of the United States, which shall consist of a Senate and House of Representatives.

SECTION 2. The House of Representatives shall be composed of members chosen every second year by the people of the several States, and the electors in each State shall have the qualifications requisite for electors of the most numerous branch of the State Legislature.

No person shall be a Representative who shall not have attained to the age of twenty-five years, and been seven years a citizen of the United States, and who shall not, when elected, be an inhabitant of that State in which he shall be chosen. Representatives and direct taxes shall be apportioned among the several States which may be included within this Union, according to their respective numbers, which shall be determined by adding to the whole number of free persons, including those bound to service for a term of years, and excluding Indians not taxed, three-fifths of all other persons. The actual enumeration shall be made within three years after the first meeting of the Congress of the United States, and within every subsequent term of ten years, in such manner as they shall by law direct. The number of representatives shall not exceed one for every thirty thousand, but each State shall have at least one Representative; and until such enumeration shall be made, the State of New Hampshire shall be entitled to choose three, Massachusetts eight, Rhode Island and Providence Plantations one, Connecticut five, New York six, New Jersey four, Pennsylvania eight, Delaware one, Maryland six, Virginia ten, North Carolina five, South Carolina five, and Georgia three. When vacancies happen in the representation from any State, the executive authority thereof shall issue writs of election to fill such vacancies. The House of Representatives shall choose their Speaker and other officers; and shall have the sole power of impeachment.

SECTION 3. The Senate of the United States shall be composed of two Senators from each State, chosen by the legislature thereof, for six years and each Senator shall have one vote. Immediately after they shall be assembled in consequence of the first election, they shall be divided as equally as may be into three classes. The seats of the Senators of the first class shall be vacated at the expiration of the second year, of the second class at the expiration of the fourth year, and of the third class at the expiration of the sixth year, so that one-third may be chosen every second year; and if vacancies happen by resignation, or otherwise, during the recess of the legislature of any State, the executive thereof may make temporary appointments until the next meeting of the legislature, which shall then fill such vacancies. No person shall be a Senator who shall not have attained to the age of thirty years, and been nine years a citizen of the United States, and who shall not, when elected, be an inhabitant of that State for which he shall be chosen. The Vice President of the United States shall be President of the Senate, but shall have no vote, unless they be equally divided. The Senate shall choose their other officers, and also a President pro tempore, in the absence of the Vice President, or when he shall exercise the office of President of the United States. The Senate shall have the sole power to try all impeachments. When sitting for that purpose, they shall be on oath or affirmation. When the President of the United States is tried, the Chief Justice shall preside: and no person shall be convicted without the concurrence of two thirds of the members present. Judgment in cases of impeachment shall not extend further than to removal from office, and disqualification to hold and enjoy any office of honor, trust or profit under the United States: but the party convicted shall nevertheless be liable and subject to indictment, trial, judgment and punishment, according to law.

SECTION 4. The times, places and manner of holding elections for Senators and Representatives, shall be prescribed in each State by the legislature thereof; but the Congress may at any time by law make or alter such regulations, except as to the places of choosing Senators. The Congress shall assemble at least once in every year, and such meeting shall be on the first Monday in December, unless they shall by law appoint a different day.

SECTION 5. Each House shall be the judge of the elections, returns and qualifications of its own members, and a majority of each shall constitute a quorum to do business; but a smaller number may adjourn from day to day, and may be authorized to compel the attendance of absent members, in such manner, and under such penalties as each House may provide. Each House may determine the rules of its proceedings, punish its members for disorderly behaviour, and, with the concurrence of two-thirds, expel a member. Each House shall keep a journal of its proceedings, and from time to time publish the same, excepting such parts as may in their judgment require secrecy; and the yeas and the nays of the members of either house on any question shall, at the desire of one-fifth of those present, be entered on the journal. Neither House, during the session of Congress, shall, without the consent of the other, adjourn for more than three days, nor to any other place than that in which the two Houses shall be sitting.

SECTION 6. The Senators and Representatives shall receive a compensation for their services, to be ascertained by law, and paid out of the Treasury of the United States. They shall in all cases, except treason, felony and breach of the peace, be privileged from arrest during their attendance at the session of their respective Houses, and in going to and returning from the same; and for any speech or debate in either House, they shall not be questioned in any other place. No Senator or Representative shall, during the time for which he was elected, be appointed to any civil office under the authority of the United States, which shall have been created, or the emoluments whereof shall have been increased during such time; and no person holding any office under the United States, shall be a member of either House during his continuance in office.

SECTION 7. All bills for raising revenue shall originate in the House of Representatives; but the Senate may propose or concur with amendments as on other bills.

Every bill which shall have passed the House of Representatives and the Senate, shall, before it becomes a law, be presented to the President of the United States; if he approves he shall sign it, but if not he shall return it, with his objections to that

House in which it shall have originated, who shall enter the objections at large on their journal, and proceed to reconsider it. If after such reconsideration two thirds of that House shall agree to pass the bill, it shall be sent, together with the objections, to the other House, by which it shall likewise be reconsidered, and if approved by two thirds of that House, it shall become a law. But in all such cases the votes of both Houses shall be determined by yeas and nays, and the names of the persons voting for and against the bill shall be entered on the journal of each House respectively. If any bill shall not be returned by the President within ten days (Sundays excepted) after it shall have been presented to him, the same shall be a law, in like manner as if he had signed it, unless the Congress by their adjournment prevent its return, in which case it shall not be a law. Every order, resolution, or vote to which the concurrence of the Senate and House of Representatives may be necessary (except on a question of adjournment) shall be presented to the President of the United States; and before the same shall take effect, shall be approved by him, or being disapproved by him, shall be repassed by two thirds of the Senate and House of Representatives, according to the rules and limitations prescribed in the case of a bill.

SECTION 8. The Congress shall have power to lay and collect taxes, duties, imposts and excises, to pay the debts and provide for the common defense and general welfare of the United States; but all duties, imposts and excises shall be uniform throughout the United States; To borrow money on the credit of the United States; To regulate commerce with foreign nations, and among the several States, and with the Indian tribes; To establish a uniform rule of naturalization, and uniform laws on the subject of bankruptcies throughout the United States; To coin money, regulate the value thereof, and of foreign coin, and fix the standard of weights and measures; To provide for the punishment of counterfeiting the securities and current coin of the United States; To establish post offices and post roads; To promote the progress of science and useful arts, by securing for limited times to authors and inventors the exclusive right to their respective writings and discoveries; To constitute tribunals inferior to the Supreme Court; To define and punish piracies and felonies committed on the high seas, and offenses against the law of nations; To declare war, grant letters of marque and reprisal, and make rules concerning captures on land and water; To raise and support armies, but no appropriation of money to that use shall be for a longer term than two years; To provide and maintain a navy; To make rules for the government and regulation of the land and naval forces; To provide for calling forth the militia to execute the laws of the Union, suppress insurrections and repel invasions; To provide for organizing, arming, and disciplining the militia, and for governing such part of them as may be employed in the service of the United States, reserving to the States respectively, the appointment of the officers, and the authority of training the militia according to the discipline prescribed by Congress; To exercise exclusive legislation in all cases whatsoever, over such district (not exceeding ten miles square) as may, by cession of particular States, and the acceptance of Congress, become the seat of the Government of the United States, and to exercise like authority over all places purchased by the consent of the legislature of the State in which the same shall be, for the erection of forts, magazines, arsenals, dock-yards, and other needful buildings; - And To make all laws which shall be necessary and proper for carrying into execution the foregoing powers, and all other powers vested by this Constitution in the Government of the United States, or in any department or officer thereof.

215

Appendices

SECTION 9. The migration or importation of such persons as any of the States now existing shall think proper to admit, shall not be prohibited by the Congress prior to the year one thousand eight hundred and eight, but a tax or duty may be imposed on such importation, not exceeding ten dollars for each person. The privilege of the writ of habeas corpus shall not be suspended, unless when in cases of rebellion or invasion the public safety may require it. No bill of attainder or ex post facto law shall be passed. No capitation, or other direct, tax shall be laid, unless in proportion to the census or enumeration herein before directed to be taken. No tax or duty shall be laid on articles exported from any State. No preference shall be given by any regulation of commerce or revenue to the ports of one State over those of another: nor shall vessels bound to, or from, one State, be obliged to enter, clear, or pay duties in another. No money shall be drawn from the Treasury, but in consequence of appropriations made by law; and a regular statement and account of the receipts and expenditures of all public money shall be published from time to time. No title of nobility shall be granted by the United States: And no person holding any office of profit or trust under them, shall, without the consent of the Congress, accept of any present, emolument, office, or title, of any kind whatever, from any King, Prince, or foreign State.

SECTION 10. No State shall enter into any treaty, alliance, or confederation; grant letters of marque and reprisal; coin money; emit bills of credit; make any thing but gold and silver coin a tender in payment of debts; pass any bill of attainder, ex post facto law, or law impairing the obligation of contracts, or grant any title of nobility. No State shall, without the consent of the Congress, lay any imposts or duties on imports or exports, except what may be absolutely necessary for executing its inspection laws: and the net produce of all duties and imposts, laid by any state on imports or exports, shall be for the use of the Treasury of the United States; and all such laws shall be subject to the revision and control of the Congress. No State shall, without the consent of Congress, lay any duty of tonnage, keep troops, or ships of war in time of peace, enter into any agreement or compact with another State, or with a foreign power, or engage in war, unless actually invaded, or in such imminent danger as will not admit of delay.

ARTICLE II

SECTION 1. The executive power shall be vested in a President of the United States of America. He shall hold his office during the term of four years, and together with the Vice President, chosen for the same term, be elected, as follows:

Each State, shall appoint, in such manner as the legislature thereof may direct, a number of electors, equal to the whole number of Senators and Representatives to which the State may be entitled in the Congress; but no Senator or Representative, or person holding an office of trust or profit under the United States, shall be appointed an elector. The electors shall meet in their respective States, and vote by ballot for two persons, of whom one at least shall not be an inhabitant of the same State with themselves. And they shall make a list of all the persons voted for, and of the number of votes for each; which list they shall sign and certify, and transmit sealed to the seat of the Government of the United States, directed to the President of the Senate. The President of the Senate shall, in the presence of the Senate and House of Representatives, open all the certificates, and the votes shall then be counted. The person having the greatest number of votes shall be the President, if such number be a majority of the whole number of electors appointed; and if there be more than one who have such majority, and have an equal number of votes, then the House of Representatives shall immediately choose by ballot one of them for President; and if no person have a majority, then from the five highest on the list the said House shall in like manner choose the President. But in choosing the President, the votes shall be taken by States, the representation from each State having one vote; a quorum for this purpose shall consist of a member or members from two thirds of the States, and a majority of all the States shall be necessary to a choice. In every case, after the choice of the President, the person having the greatest number of votes of the electors shall be the Vice President. But if there should remain two or more who have equal votes, the Senate shall choose from them by ballot the Vice President. The Congress may determine the time of choosing the electors, and the day on which they shall give their votes; which day shall be the same throughout the United States. No person except a natural born citizen, or a citizen of the United States, at the time of the adoption of this Constitution, shall be eligible to the office of President; neither shall any person be eligible to that office who shall not have attained to the age of thirty-five years, and been fourteen years a resident within the United States. In case of the removal of the President from office, or of his death, resignation, or inability to discharge the powers and duties of the said office, the same shall devolve on the Vice President, and the Congress may by law provide for the case of removal, death, resignation, or inability, both of the President and Vice President, declaring what officer shall then act as President, and such officer shall act accordingly, until the disability be removed, or a President be elected. The President shall, at stated times, receive for his services, a compensation, which shall neither be increased nor diminished during the period for which he shall have been elected, and he shall not receive within that period any other emolument from the United States, or any of them. Before he enter on the execution of his office, he shall take the following oath or affirmation: - "I do solemnly swear (or affirm) that I will faithfully execute the office of President of the United States, and will to the best of my ability, preserve, protect and defend the Constitution of the United States."

SECTION 2. The President shall be Commander in Chief of the Army and Navy of the United States, and of the militia of the several States, when called into the actual service of the United States; he may require the opinion, in writing, of the principal officer in each of the executive departments, upon any subject relating to the duties of their respective offices, and he shall have power to grant reprieves and pardons for offenses against the United States, except in cases of impeachment. He shall have power, by and with the advice and consent of the Senate, to make treaties, provided two thirds of the Senators present concur; and he shall nominate, and by and with the advice and consent of the Senate, shall appoint ambassadors, other public ministers and consuls, Judges of the Supreme Court, and all other officers of the United States, whose appointments are not herein otherwise provided for, and which shall be established by law: but the Congress may by law vest the appointment of such inferior officers, as they think proper, in the President alone, in the courts of law, or in the heads of departments. The President shall have power to fill up all vacancies that may happen during the recess of the Senate, by granting commissions which shall expire at the end of their next session.

SECTION 3. He shall from time to time give to the Congress information of the

State of the Union, and recommend to their consideration such measures as he shall judge necessary and expedient; he may, on extraordinary occasions, convene both Houses, or either of them, and in case of disagreement between them, with respect to the time of adjournment, he may adjourn them to such time as he shall think proper; he shall receive ambassadors and other public ministers; he shall take care that the laws be faithfully executed, and shall commission all the officers of the United States.

SECTION 4. The President, Vice President and all civil officers of the United States, shall be removed from office on impeachment for, and conviction of, treason, bribery, or other high crimes and misdemeanors.

ARTICLE III

SECTION 1. The judicial power of the United States, shall be vested in one Supreme Court, and in such inferior courts as the Congress may from time to time ordain and establish. The judges, both of the Supreme and inferior Courts, shall hold their offices during good behaviour, and shall, at stated times, receive for their services, a compensation, which shall not be diminished during their continuance in office.

SECTION 2. The judicial power shall extend to all cases, in law and equity, arising under this Constitution, the laws of the United States, and treaties made, or which shall be made, under their authority; - to all cases affecting ambassadors, other public ministers and consuls; - to all cases of admiralty and maritime jurisdiction; - to controversies to which the United States shall be a party; - to controversies between two or more States; - between a State and citizens of another State; - between citizens of different States, - between citizens of the same State claiming lands under grants of different States, and between a State, or the citizens thereof, and foreign States, citizens or subjects.

In all cases affecting ambassadors, other public ministers and consuls, and those in which a State shall be a party, the Supreme Court shall have original jurisdiction. In all the other cases before mentioned, the Supreme Court shall have appellate jurisdiction, both as to law and fact, with such exceptions, and under such regulations as the Congress shall make. The trial of all crimes, except in cases of impeachment, shall be by jury; and such trial shall be held in the State where the said crimes shall have been committed; but when not committed within any State, the trial shall be at such place or places as the Congress may by law have directed.

SECTION 3. Treason against the United States, shall consist only in levying war against them, or in adhering to their enemies, giving them aid and comfort. No person shall be convicted of treason unless on the testimony of two witnesses to the same overt act, or on confession in open court. The Congress shall have power to declare the punishment of treason, but no attainder of treason shall work corruption of blood, or forfeiture except during the life of the person attainted.

ARTICLE IV

SECTION 1. Full faith and credit shall be given in each State to the public acts, records, and judicial proceedings of every other State. And the Congress may by general laws prescribe the manner in which such acts, records, and proceedings shall be proved, and the effect thereof.

SECTION 2. The citizens of each State shall be entitled to all privileges and immunities of citizens in the several States. A person charged in any State with treason, felony, or other crime, who shall flee from justice, and be found in another State, shall on demand of the executive authority of the State from which he fled, be delivered up, to be removed to the State having jurisdiction of the crime. No person held to service or labour in one State, under the laws thereof, escaping into another, shall, in consequence of any law or regulation therein, be discharged from such service or labour, but shall be delivered up on claim of the party to whom such service or labour may be due.

SECTION 3. New States may be admitted by the Congress into this Union; but no new State shall be formed or erected within the jurisdiction of any other State; nor any State be formed by the junction of two or more States, or parts of States, without the consent of the legislatures of the States concerned as well as of the Congress. The Congress shall have power to dispose of and make all needful rules and regulations respecting the Territory or other property belonging to the United States; and nothing in this Constitution shall be so construed as to prejudice any claims of the United States, or of any particular State.

SECTION 4. The United States shall guarantee to every State in this Union a republican form of Government, and shall protect each of them against invasion; and on application of the legislature, or of the executive (when the legislature cannot be convened) against domestic violence.

ARTICLE V

The Congress, whenever two thirds of both Houses shall deem it necessary, shall propose amendments to this Constitution, or on the application of the legislatures of two thirds of the several States, shall call a convention for proposing amendments, which, in either case, shall be valid to all intents and purposes, as part of this Constitution, when ratified by the legislatures of three fourths of the several States, or by conventions in three fourths thereof, as the one or the other mode of ratification may be proposed by the Congress; provided that no amendment which may be made prior to the year one thousand eight hundred and eight shall in any manner affect the first and fourth clauses in the Ninth Section of the First Article; and that no State, without its consent, shall be deprived of its equal suffrage in the Senate.

ARTICLE VI

All debts contracted and engagements entered into, before the adoption of this Constitution, shall be as valid against the United States under this Constitution, as under the Confederation.

This Constitution, and the laws of the United States which shall be made in pursuance thereof; and all treaties made, or which shall be made, under the authority of the United States, shall be the supreme law of the land; and the judges in every State shall be bound thereby, any thing in the Constitution or laws of any State to the contrary notwithstanding. The Senators and Representatives before mentioned, and the members of the several State legislatures, and all executive and judicial officers, both of the United States and of the several States, shall be bound by oath or affirmation, to support this Constitution; but no religious test shall ever be required as a qualification to any office or public trust under the United States.

ARTICLE VII

The ratification of the conventions of nine States shall be sufficient for the establishment of this Constitution between the States so ratifying the same. Done in convention by the unanimous consent of the States present the seventeenth day of September in the year of our Lord one thousand seven hundred and eighty seven and of the independence of the United States of America the twelfth. In witness whereof we have hereunto subscribed our names,

(signers)

Amendments

(The first ten amendments to the Constitution are called the Bill of Rights and were adopted in 1791.)

ARTICLE I

Congress shall make no law respecting an establishment of religion, or prohibiting the free exercise thereof; or abridging the freedom of speech, or of the press; or the right of the people peaceably to assemble, and to petition the Government for a redress of grievances.

ARTICLE II

A well regulated militia, being necessary to the security of a free State, the right of the people to keep and bear arms, shall not be infringed.

ARTICLE III

No soldier shall, in time of peace be quartered in any house, without the consent of the owner, nor in time of war, but in a manner to be prescribed by law.

ARTICLE IV

The right of the people to be secure in their persons, houses, papers, and effects, against unreasonable searches and seizures, shall not be violated, and no warrants shall issue, but upon probable cause, supported by oath or affirmation, and particularly describing the place to be searched, and the persons or things to be seized.

ARTICLE V

No person shall be held to answer for a capital, or otherwise infamous crime, unless on a presentment or indictment of a Grand Jury, except in cases arising in the land or naval forces, or in the militia, when in actual service in time of war or public danger; nor shall any person be subject for the same offense to be twice put in jeopardy of life or limb; nor shall be compelled in any criminal case to be a witness against himself, nor be deprived of life, liberty, or property, without due process of law; nor shall private property be taken for public use, without just compensation.

ARTICLE VI

In all criminal prosecutions, the accused shall enjoy the right to a speedy and public trial, by an impartial jury of the State and district wherein the crime shall have been committed, which district shall have been previously ascertained by law, and to be informed of the nature and cause of the accusation; to be confronted with the witnesses against him; to have compulsory process for obtaining witnesses in his favor, and to have the assistance of counsel for his defense.

ARTICLE VII

In suits at common law, where the value in controversy shall exceed twenty dollars, the right of trial by jury shall be preserved, and no fact tried by a jury, shall be otherwise reexamined in any Court of the United States, than according to the rules of the common law.

ARTICLE VIII

Excessive bail shall not be required, nor excessive fines imposed, nor cruel and unusual punishments inflicted.

ARTICLE IX

The enumeration in the Constitution, of certain rights, shall not be construed to deny or disparage others retained by the people.

ARTICLE X

The powers not delegated to the United States by the Constitution, nor prohibited by it to the States, are reserved to the States respectively, or to the people.

ARTICLE XI

The judicial power of the United States shall not be construed to extend to any suit in law or equity, commenced or prosecuted against one of the United States by citizens of another State, or by citizens or subjects of any foreign State.

ARTICLE XII

The electors shall meet in their respective States, and vote by ballot for President and Vice President, one of whom, at least, shall not be an inhabitant of the same State with themselves; they shall name in their ballots the person voted for as President, and in distinct ballots the person voted for as Vice President, and they shall make distinct lists of all persons voted for as President, and of all persons voted for as Vice President, and of the number of votes for each, which lists they shall sign and certify, and transmit sealed to the seat of the government of the United States, directed to the President of the Senate; - The President of the Senate shall, in the presence of the Senate and House of Representatives, open all the certificates and the votes shall then be counted; The person having the greatest number of votes for President, shall be the President, if such number be a majority of the whole number of electors appointed; and if no person have such majority, then from the persons having the highest numbers not exceeding three on the list of those voted for as President, the House of Representatives shall choose immediately, by ballot, the President. But in choosing the President, the votes shall be taken by States, the representation from each State having one vote; a quorum for this purpose shall consist of a member or members from two-thirds of the States, and a majority of all the States shall be necessary of a choice. And if the House of Representatives shall not choose a President whenever the right of choice shall devolve upon them, before the fourth day of March next following, then the Vice President shall act as President, as in the case of the death or other constitutional disability of the President. - The person having the greatest number of votes as Vice President, shall be the Vice President, if such number be a majority of the whole number of electors appointed, and if no person have a majority, then from the two highest numbers on the list, the Senate shall choose the Vice President; a quorum for the purpose shall consist of two-thirds of the whole number of Senators, and a majority of the whole number shall be necessary to a choice. But no person constitutionally ineligible to the office of President shall be eligible to that of Vice President of the United States.

ARTICLE XIII

SECTION 1. Neither slavery nor involuntary servitude, except as a punishment for crime whereof the party shall have been duly convicted, shall exist within the United States, or any place subject to their jurisdiction.

SECTION 2. Congress shall have power to enforce this article by appropriate legislation.

ARTICLE XIV

SECTION 1. All persons born or naturalized in the United States, and subject to the jurisdiction thereof, are citizens of the United States and of the State wherein they reside. No State shall make or enforce any law which shall abridge the privileges or immunities of citizens of the United States; nor shall any State deprive any person of life, liberty, or property, without due process of law; nor deny to any person within its jurisdiction the equal protection of the laws.

SECTION 2. Representatives shall be apportioned among the several States according to their respective numbers, counting the whole number of persons in each State, excluding Indians not taxed. But when the right to vote at any election for the choice of electors for President and Vice President of the United States, Representatives in Congress, the executive and judicial officers of a State, or the members of the legislature thereof, is denied to any of the male inhabitants of such State, being twenty-one years of age, and citizens of the United States, or in any way abridged, except for participation in rebellion, or other crime, the basis of representation therein shall be reduced in the proportion which the number of such male citizens shall bear to the whole number of male citizens twenty-one years of age in such State.

SECTION 3. No person shall be a Senator or Representative in Congress, or elector of President and Vice President, or hold any office, civil or military, under the United States, or under any State, who, having previously taken an oath, as a member of Congress, or as an officer of the United States, or as a member of any State legislature, or as an executive or judicial officer of any State, to support the Constitution of the United States, shall have engaged in insurrection or rebellion against the same, or given aid or comfort to the enemies thereof. But Congress may by a vote of two-thirds of each house, remove such disability.

SECTION 4. The validity of the public debt of the United States, authorized by law, including debts incurred for payment of pensions and bounties for services in suppressing insurrection or rebellion, shall not be questioned. But neither the United States nor any State shall assume or pay any debt or obligation incurred in aid of insurrection or rebellion against the United States, or any claim for the loss or emancipation of any slave; but all such debts, obligations and claims shall be held illegal and void.

SECTION 5. The Congress shall have power to enforce, by appropriate legislation, the provisions of this article.

ARTICLE XV

SECTION 1. The right of citizens of the United States to vote shall not be denied or abridged by the United States or by any State on account of race, color, or previous condition of servitude.

SECTION 2. The Congress shall have power to enforce this article by appropriate legislation.

ARTICLE XVI

The Congress shall have power to lay and collect taxes on incomes, from whatever source derived, without apportionment among the several States, and without regard to any census or enumeration.

ARTICLE XVII

SECTION 1. The Senate of the United States shall be composed of two Senators from each State, elected by the people thereof, for six years; and each Senator shall have one vote. The electors in each State shall have the qualifications requisite for electors of the most numerous branch of the State legislatures.

SECTION 2. When vacancies happen in the representation of any State in the Senate, the executive authority of such State shall issue writs of election to fill such vacancies: Provided, that the legislature of any State may empower the executive thereof to make temporary appointments until the people fill the vacancies by election as the legislature may direct.

SECTION 3. This amendment shall not be so construed as to affect the election or term of any Senator chosen before it becomes valid as part of the Constitution.

ARTICLE XVIII

SECTION 1. After one year from the ratification of this article the manufacture, sale, or transportation of intoxicating liquors within, the importation thereof into, or the exportation thereof from the United States and all territory subject to the jurisdiction thereof for beverage purposes is hereby prohibited.

SECTION 2. The Congress and the several States shall have concurrent power to enforce this article by appropriate legislation.

SECTION 3. This article shall be inoperative unless it shall have been ratified as an amendment to the Constitution by the legislatures of the several States, as provided in the Constitution, within seven years from the date of the submission hereof to the States by the Congress.

ARTICLE XIX

SECTION 1. The right of citizens of the United States to vote shall not be denied or abridged by the United States or by any State on account of sex.

SECTION 2. Congress shall have power to enforce this article by appropriate legislation.

ARTICLE XX

SECTION 1. The terms of the President and Vice President shall end at noon on the 20th day of January, and the terms of Senators and Representatives at noon on the 3d day of January, of the years in which such terms would have ended if this article had not been ratified; and the terms of their successors shall then begin.

SECTION 2. The Congress shall assemble at least once in every year, and such meeting shall begin at noon on the 3d day of January, unless they shall by law appoint a different day.

SECTION 3. If, at the time fixed for the beginning of the term of the President, the President elect shall have died, the Vice President elect shall become President. If a President shall not have been chosen before the time fixed for the beginning of his term, or if the President elect shall have failed to qualify, then the Vice President elect shall act as President until a President shall have qualified; and the Congress may by law provide for the case wherein neither a President elect nor a Vice President elect shall have qualified, declaring who shall then act as President, or the manner in which one who is to act shall be selected, and such person shall act accordingly until a

President or Vice President shall have qualified.

SECTION 4. The Congress may by law provide for the case of the death of any of the persons from whom the House of Representatives may choose a President whenever the right of choice shall have devolved upon them, and for the case of the death of any of the persons from whom the Senate may choose a Vice President whenever the right of choice shall have devolved upon them.

SECTION 5. Sections 1 and 2 shall take effect on the 15th day of October following the ratification of this article.

SECTION 6. This article shall be inoperative unless it shall have been ratified as an amendment to the Constitution by the legislatures of three-fourths of the several States within seven years from the date of its submission.

ARTICLE XXI

SECTION 1. The eighteenth article of amendment to the Constitution of the United States is hereby repealed.

SECTION 2. The transportation or importation into any State, Territory, or possession of the United States for delivery or use therein of intoxicating liquors, in violation of the laws thereof, is hereby prohibited.

SECTION 3. This article shall be inoperative unless it shall have been ratified as an amendment to the Constitution by conventions in the several States, as provided in the Constitution, within seven years from the date of the submission hereof to the States by the Congress.

ARTICLE XXII

SECTION 1. No person shall be elected to the office of the President more than twice, and no person who has held the office of President, or acted as President, for more than two years of a term to which some other person was elected President shall be elected to the office of the President more than once. But this article shall not apply to any person holding the office of President when this article was proposed by the Congress, and shall not prevent any person who may be holding the office of President, or acting as President, during the term within which this article becomes operative from holding the office of President or acting as President during the remainder of such term.

SECTION 2. This article shall be inoperative unless it shall have been ratified as an amendment to the Constitution by the legislatures of three-fourths of the several States within seven years from the date of its submission to the States by the Congress.

ARTICLE XXIII

SECTION 1. The District constituting the seat of Government of the United States shall appoint in such manner as the Congress may direct: A number of electors of President and Vice President equal to the whole number of Senators and Representatives in Congress to which the District would be entitled if it were a State, but in no event more than the least populous State; they shall be in addition to those appointed by the States, but they shall be considered, for the purposes of the election of President and Vice President, to be electors appointed by a State; and they shall meet in the District and perform such duties as provided by the twelfth article of amendment.

SECTION 2. The Congress shall have power to enforce this article by appropriate legislation.

ARTICLE XXIV

SECTION 1. The right of citizens of the United States to vote in any primary or other election for President or Vice President, for electors for President or Vice President, or for Senator or Representative in Congress, shall not be denied or abridged by the United States or any State by reason of failure to pay any poll tax or other tax.

SECTION 2. The Congress shall have power to enforce this article by appropriate legislation.

ARTICLE XXV

SECTION 1. In case of the removal of the President from office or of his death or resignation, the Vice President shall become President.

SECTION 2. Whenever there is a vacancy in the office of the Vice President, the President shall nominate a Vice President who shall take office upon confirmation by a majority vote of both Houses of Congress.

SECTION 3. Whenever the President transmits to the President pro tempore of the Senate and the Speaker of the House of Representatives his written declaration that he is unable to discharge the powers and duties of his office, and until he transmits to them a written declaration to the contrary, such powers and duties shall be discharged by the Vice President as Acting President.

SECTION 4. Whenever the Vice President and a majority of either the principal officers of the executive departments or of such other body as Congress may by law provide, transmit to the President pro tempore of the Senate and the Speaker of the House of Representatives their written declaration that the President is unable to discharge the powers and duties of his office, the Vice President shall immediately assume the powers and duties of the office as Acting President.

Thereafter, when the President transmits to the President pro tempore of the Senate and the Speaker of the House of Representatives his written declaration that no inability exists, he shall resume the powers and duties of his office unless the Vice President and a majority of either the principal officers of the executive department or of such other body as Congress may by law provide, transmit within four days to the President pro tempore of the Senate and the Speaker of the House of Representatives their written declaration that the President is unable to discharge the powers and duties of his office. Thereupon Congress shall decide the issue, assembling within forty-eight hours for that purpose if not in session. If the Congress, within twenty-one days after receipt of the latter written declaration, or, if Congress is not in session, within twenty-one days after Congress is required to assemble, determines by two-thirds vote of both Houses that the President is unable to discharge the powers and duties of his office, the Vice President shall continue to discharge the same as Acting President; otherwise, the President shall resume the powers and duties of his office.

ARTICLE XXVI

SECTION 1. The right of citizens of the United States who are 18 years of age or older, to vote shall not be denied or abridged by the United States or by any State on account of age.

Appendix E
"Change the World Training"

Most of us do not really know what we want. We are trained by advertisers to drink beer, buy cars, not eat fats, and so on. The motivations are generally based on fear, envy, greed, lust, and other negative influences. We may not understand the mental fog in which we exist but others (advertisers) do.

The basic assumption inherent in "Change the World Training" is to burn off the fog. No longer will you simply react without knowing why. Our goal is for each belief, emotion, and action you experience to be fully conscious. Although the formal training itself is relatively short, only three days, the training process to which you will be introduced is never-ending. All of your most basic, and sometimes unconscious, beliefs will be challenged.

DAY ONE: ME, MYSELF

This portion of the training is a facilitated series of exercises designed to make you pay attention to what you believe and how those beliefs effect the reality you experience. You will be shown simple techniques to help you adopt, reinforce, and change beliefs. These techniques can also be used to help you achieve goals you set for yourself for the rest of your life. During Day One, you will begin to decide what to do with the rest of your life, what kind of person you want to be, and how to constantly improve your day-to-day experience.

DAY TWO: CANDIDATES, ELECTIONS, AND HOW TO WIN.

This portion of the training introduces you to a variety of communication skills which you can use to put people into office, deal with them once they are in office, and achieve your political goals. While concentrating on the context of government, these techniques will also help you in your daily struggle for the legal tender.

Training will be supplemented by extensive written materials, explanations, how-to manuals and videos. The written materials will be yours to keep.

You will be given access to the tools you will need to succeed in "Changing the World." You will meet others who share your interests. From the point of view of the people who are making a mess of our country, our economy, and our lives, you will be armed and dangerous.

DAY THREE: WHAT NOW?

The third day of "Change the World Training" will show you how to apply the skills and tools you will have gained during the first and second days of Training. This will involve two additional tools: The Focus Plan Protocol and a Team Building Process.

The Focus Plan Protocol is a technique to guide you through the steps necessary to assure that you take into account and deal successfully with all the various factors and issues which can cause you to fail. You will learn how to identify all of the elements inherent in the situation confronting you. You will be shown how to set attainable objectives. You will be given a set of gut-level questions to prepare you for all of the obstacles to success you may encounter. Finally, you will receive an introduction to "positioning," the mechanism by which you can define your issue, product, or candidate in terms which appeal to the perceived wants and needs of your audience, market, or electorate.

I was introduced to the Focus Plan Protocol process by Frank Callahan. I discussed him earlier in the context of Duncan Hines cake mix. This is the process he uses to break out of the linear thinking that often links us to failure.

The Team Building Process will help you to turn those people you are working with into a cohesive, effective unit. The technique was introduced to me by a management consultant named Kevin Hart who has successfully used it for a variety of clients in distressed business situations, to allow them to survive.

The net result of "Change the World Training" is to equip you to change the world. All of us are dissatisfied with the status quo for one reason or another. But we allow ourselves to be victims of the system, victims of various institutions, or victims of our bosses, spouses, or family members.

We think we pay too much in taxes. We think we receive too little in services. The society appears to be on the verge of disaster. Dirty air, global warming, holes in the ozone, drugs in our schools, crime, corruption, and unbeatable foreign economic competition seem to overwhelm us. Who owns these problems?

Senators, Representatives, the President, the Mayor, the school board—each of these people and institutions own the problem. But, so do each of us! What are you doing to make the world a better, safer, cleaner place to live?

"Change the World Training" addresses that question. Now, you can do more than complain. How much more is up to you. There are no limits to what you can do with the skills, tools, and processes you will be given.

Appendix F
For Further Reading

Abboud, Robert A. *Money in the Bank: How Safe Is It?*
(Homewood, Illinois, Dow Jones-Irwin, 1988).

Bernstein, Carl and Woodward, Bob. *All the President's Men.*
(New York, Simon & Schuster, 1974).

Burke, James. *The Day the Universe Changed*
(Boston, Little, Brown and Co., 1985)

Campbell, Joseph. *Transformations of Myth Through Time.*
(New York, Perennial Library, 1990).

Campbell, Joseph and Moyers, Bill. *The Power of Myth.*
(New York, Doubleday, 1988).

Collier, Peter and Horowitz, David. *Destructive Generation: Second Thoughts About the 60's.* (New York, Summit Books, 1989).

Copeland, Doug. *Generation X.*
(New York, St. Martin's Press, 1991).

Covey, Stephen R. *The Seven Habits of Highly Effective People: Restoring the Character Ethic.*
(New York, Simon & Schuster, 1989).

Corcoran, James. *Bitter Harvest.* (New York, Viking, 1990).

Deaver, Michael K. with Herskowitz, Mickey. *Behind the Scenes.*
(New York, Morrow, 1987).

Drucker, Peter F. *Innovation and Entrepreneurship: Practice and Principles.* (New York, Harper & Row, 1985).

Drucker, Peter F. *The New Realities: In Government and Politics, In Economics and Business, In Society and World View.*
(New York, Harper & Row, 1989).

Gleick, James. *Chaos: Making a New Science.*
(New York, Viking, 1987).

Greider, William. *Secrets of the Temple: How the Federal Reserve Runs the Country.* (New York, Simon & Schuster, 1987).

Greenfield, Jeff and Newfield, Jack. *A Populist Manifesto: The Making of a New Majority.* (New York, Praeger, 1972).

Halberstam, David. *The Reckoning.*
(New York, William Morrow and Company, 1986).

Hayek, F.A. *The Fatal Conceit: The Errors of Socialism.*
(Chicago, University of Chicago Press, 1988).

Hickel, Walter J. *Who Owns America.*
(Edgewood Cliffs, NJ, Prentice-Hall, 1971).

Johnson, Paul. *Modern Times: The World from the Twenties
to the Eighties.*(New York, Harper & Row, 1983).

Locke, John. *An Essay Concerning Human Understanding.*
(London, England, J.M. Dent & Sons, Ltd., 1961).

Locke, John. *The Second Treatise of Government.*
(New York, The Bobbs-Merril Co., Inc., 1952).

Marrs, Jim. *Crossfire: The Plot that Killed Kennedy.*
(New York, Carroll & Graf, 1989).

Moyers, Bill. *A World of Ideas: Conversations with Thoughtful
Men and Women About American Life Today and the Ideas
Shaping Our Future.* (New York, Doubleday, 1989).

Newton, Maxwell. *The Fed.* (New York, Times Books, 1983).

Novak, Michael. *The Spirit of Democratic Capitalism.*
(New York, Simon & Schuster, 1982).

Pascale, Richard Tanner. *Managing on the Edge.*
(New York, Simon & Schuster, 1990).

Peck, M. Scott. *The Different Drum: Community-making and Peace.*
(New York, Simon & Schuster, 1987).

Peck, M. Scott. *The Road Less Traveled.*
(New York, Simon & Schuster, 1978).

Peters, Tom. *Thriving on Chaos: A Handbook for a Management
Revolution.* (New York, Randon House, 1987).

Peters, Tom. *A Passion for Excellence.*
(New York, Warner Books, 1985).

Phillips, Kevin P. *The Politics of Rich and Poor: Wealth and the
American Electorate in the Reagan Aftermath.*
(New York, Random House, 1990).

Reich, Robert B. *The Work of Nations: Preparing Ourselves for 21st
Century Capitalism.* (New York, A.A. Knopf, 1991).

Schumacher, B.F. *Small is Beautiful.* (New York, Harper, 1989).

Smith, Adam (1723-1790). *The Wealth of Nations, Books I-III.*
(London, England, Penguin Group, 1986).

Smith, Adam (1930-). *Paper Money.* (Boston, G.K. Hall, 1981).

Smith, Adam (1930-). *The Roaring 80's.*
(New York, Summit Books, 1988).

Thornton, Robert M. *Cogitations from Albert Jay Nock.*
(Irvington-on-Hudson, N.Y., The Nockian Society, 1985).

Udall, Morris K. *Too Funny To Be President.*
(New York, H. Holt, 1988).

Walters, charles Jr. *Raw Materials Economics.*
(Kansas City, MO, Acres U.S.A., 1991)

Walters, Charles Jr. *Unforgiven.*
(Kansas City, MO, Economic Library, 1971).

Weaver, Henry Grady. *The Mainspring of Human Progress.*
(Irvington-on-Hudson, NY, Foundation for Economic Education,
Inc., 1953).

Wills, Garry. *Explaining America: The Federalist.*
(Garden City, NY, Doubleday, 1981).

Wills, Garry. *Inventing America: Jefferson's Declaration of
Independence.*(Garden City, NY, Doubleday, 1978).

Woodward, Bob. *The Final Days.*
(New York, Simon & Schuster, 1976).

YOUR THOUGHTS AND REACTIONS ARE
WELCOME AND APPRECIATED

Michael Foudy
P. O. Box 329
Falls Church, VA 22040-0329

Wiconi gluonihan pi na wolakota.

My rough translation of the Lakota Sioux
dedication:

Respect your life, live in friendship, and apply
these principles to all in the nation.

TAKE BACK AMERICA

MAKE YOUR VIEWS KNOWN TO CONGRESS

JOIN VOTERS OF AMERICA

Voters of America is a private non-profit, non-partisan organization, created to carry the voice of its members to the U.S. House of Representatives and the U.S. Senate. Members are able to "cast their vote" on important issues by sending a "Concerns and Opinions" form to our office. The results will be summarized and sent in letter form to your Congresspersons and Senators and to the appropriate Committee chair or Congressional leader who can promote your views. If you are interested in helping the organization grow, please fill out and send in the membership form below along with a $35 check or money order. (It is a tax-deductible contribution.)

MEMBERSHIP FORM

Name:_____

Address:_____

_____

Telephone (optional):_____

Social Security #:_____

One-time Donation of:_____

Return to:

Legislative Office: Grassroots Headquarters:
Voters of America   Voters of America
Suite 700   P.O. Box 100(Atlanta)
601 Pennsylvania Ave., NW   Waco, GA 30182
Washington, DC 20004

Please enclose $35 check or money order made payable to Voters of America (your contribution is tax-deductible).

These are the times that try men's souls. The summer soldier and the sunshine patriot will, in this crisis, shrink from the service of his country; but he that stands it now deserves the love and thanks of man and woman. Tyranny, like Hell, is not easily conquered; yet we have this consolation with us, that the harder the conflict, the more glorious the triumph.

—Thomas Paine, 1776

Stand up now to enact term limitations, rescue our economy with fair trade, sound money and parity pricing for raw materials.

Each of us has within us the ability to provide the answer, rescue America and assure a future for our children.

Join today. The Institute for American Democracy is organizing campaign committees, committees of correspondence, and providing training so that you can use the tools previously held only by political professionals to free yourself from economic and political domination and realize real power in your personal life, your community, your state and your country.

NAME_____

STREET_____

CITY/STATE/ZIP_____

PHONE NUMBER ( ) DAY ( ) NIGHT_____

Return this membership form together with your check for $120 (first year's membership fee) payable to:

Institute for American Democracy
6991 East Camelback Road, Suite B-101
Scottsdale, Arizona 85251

Membership entitles you to our monthly newsletter, access to the services of the Institute, training discounts, and a free copy of the new book *Reinventing America*.

You will be contacted within three weeks of the time your check is received to begin organizing in your community to save our country. Act now!

WALT WHITMAN'S ADVICE ON HOW TO LIVE

FOR YOUR CONSIDERATION

"THIS IS WHAT YOU SHALL DO:

Love the earth and sun and the animals, despise riches, give alms to everyone that asks, stand up for the stupid and crazy, devote your income and labor to others, hate tyrants, argue not concerning God, have patience and indulgence towards the people, take off your hat to nothing known or unknown or to any man or number of men...re-examine all you have been told at school or church or in any book, dismiss whatever insults your own soul, and your very flesh shall be a great poem."

Walt Whitman
1855